Cars we Loved in the 1950s

GILES CHAPMAN

The
History
Press

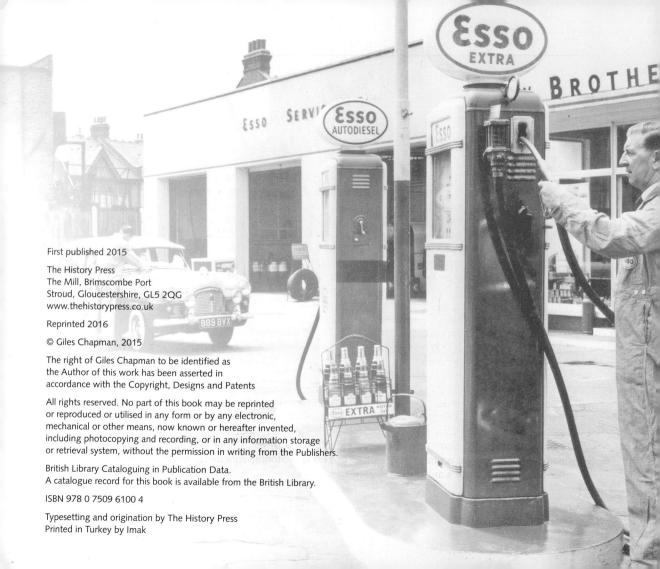

First published 2015

The History Press
The Mill, Brimscombe Port
Stroud, Gloucestershire, GL5 2QG
www.thehistorypress.co.uk

Reprinted 2016

British Library Cataloguing in Publication Data.
A catalogue record for this book is available from the British Library.

ISBN 978 0 7509 6100 4

Typesetting and origination by The History Press
Printed in Turkey by Imak

Introduction

When I set out to write this book, I wanted to bring the essence of 1950s British motoring alive again.

It was a period beginning in the rationed, restricted, make-do-and-mend austerity of the post-war era, and ending in neon-lit consumerism, motorways, foreign travel, whitewall tyres and sheer driving enjoyment. No on-road decade has ever seen such contrasts; just look at the upright and plain Vauxhall Wyvern of 1948 (page 38) and the sleek, two-tone, American-influenced Vauxhall PA Cresta of exactly ten years later (page 146), and you'll recognise how far motorists' expectations raced ahead.

However, you can't consider the 1950s British motoring scene without including the five later years of the '40s, when the car industry slowly got back on its feet. Plenty of cars now regarded as '50s icons, like the Morris Minor and Sunbeam-Talbot 90, were conceived then but only became familiar in the following decade when British drivers were allowed actually to buy new cars and the pressure to 'Export or Die' was lifted.

In this book we revisit the fifty most important and popular cars in chronological order, vividly illustrating how technology and design rapidly advanced to make them faster, stronger, safer and more attractive.

We begin with the very first post-war models and finish in 1958, when the last cars to be launched this decade actually made an impact in it. For late-period models that were really stars of the 1960s, there's a round-up chapter at the end.

Picture-researching *Cars we Loved in the 1950s* has been fascinating, and I think you'll enjoy the wealth of illustrations we've been able to cram in. A note of thanks to Linda Barnes, who supplied an interesting folder of period motoring ephemera, much of which has added to this book's authentic 1950s flavour.

Giles Chapman

Riley RM Series, 1946

The Riley RM series was one of the very first all-new British cars launched after the Second World War, and as a sports saloon it was a highly desirable property. Nonetheless, it was essentially a late 1930s design with a steel body whose supporting framework was wooden and whose roof was of stretched fabric.

Sporting 1930s Rileys had been superbly designed and engineered for driving enjoyment, though, and the RM extended this illustrious reputation without offering anything too radical. The chassis was structurally stiff, with all the seats inside the wheelbase for good ride comfort, there was torsion-bar independent front suspension, and the precise-feeling steering was by rack and pinion.

The four-cylinder engines in these cars were a couple of cuts above the average. Both the 1.5-litre (in the RMA) and the 2.5-litre (RMB) were superb twin-camshaft units in the Riley custom (although the company was now owned by Morris), and the bigger engine, with the longest stroke of any post-war British production car, produced plenty of torque and so made it particularly capable as a long-distance cruiser, able to burble along all day at 80mph. It was enhanced in 1948 when maximum power increased from 90 to 100bhp. Top speed was then a heady 95mph, and the floor-mounted gear change felt slick and accurate.

For the time, the RM offered delightful handling, although the steering – confidence inspiring on the move – was heavy work when parking.

Super to drive, the RMs' handsome, well-balanced lines still looked good in 1955 when the last RME (an updated RMA without running boards and, by then, vastly better hydraulic brakes) was built. The old-fashioned construction allowed other body styles on the same chassis, including an elegant drophead Coupé, a Roadster with three-abreast seating and a column-mounted gear lever to accommodate the middle passenger's legs, and several designs of estate car.

The handsome lines of the Riley RM saloon clothed a car with masses of driver appeal.

Summer days in the Home Counties – Riley advertising appealed to the well-heeled.

WHO LOVED IT?

There was plenty of grumbling from connoisseurs that car design during the '30s had gone to the dogs as manufacturers, such as Sunbeam, cut costs to go mass market. But in the Riley RM, sporting standards, good looks and fine road manners were maintained. The downside was twice a Morris Oxford's price, so its delights were only available to the moneyed upper-middle classes.

What they said at the time

'Overriding everything else is the astonishment that so much useable road performance can be offered for so relatively low a price ... The steering of the car gives the driver a complete feeling of confidence' – *The Motor* magazine in 1950 on the £1,224 2.5-litre saloon.

This rakish three-seater roadster version of the Riley was designed principally for the US market.

Ford V8 Pilot, 1947

In the spirit of equality with which he put the planet on wheels with the Model T, Henry Ford brought effortless power to the motoring public with the world's first mass-produced V8 engine in 1932. The idea of two banks of four cylinders at an angle to each other, in this case 60°, wasn't new, but Ford churned out these premium engines in the tens of thousands. The 3.6-litre, all-iron, side-valve motor had but a single carburettor, and just 65bhp, but it was immensely flexible, and formed the basis of the nascent American hot-rod scene. A Ford V8 Roadster also won the 1936 Monte Carlo Rally.

British-made Ford V8 saloons of the '30s had used a weedy 2.2-

This unusual metal-bodied V8 Pilot estate car was offered by the Dagenham factory but was for export only.

litre version, but the bigger engine returned in the chunky Pilot saloon in 1947, now with horsepower up to a healthy 85bhp at 3,800rpm. Forgiving and powerful with a three-speed gearbox, the car just loved loping along at 60mph in top gear, taking steep hills in its relaxed stride, and emitting a satisfying burbling sound through its exhaust pipe. Yet

it was unstressed enough to offer an easy 20mpg.

Rover and Humber drivers turned their noses up at it, and the decidedly plebeian £585 Pilot was extremely cheap, with a fake wood plastic dashboard and leatherette seats, although it did come with a built-in jacking system, a heater, rear-window blind and an opening windscreen. For just £36 more you could get the De Luxe spec with leather upholstery, radio, two loudspeakers and a built-in aerial.

Definitely something a bit 'black market' about the V8 Pilot – easy performance and a lot of metal for your money.

What they said at the time

'One can move off from rest by using first gear for just a few yards to get the car underway ... then pass straight into top, ignoring second. The Pilot will thread its way through the streets of a country market town under control of the throttle and brake pedals alone, and as soon as it is clear of the built-up area soar into the seventies' – *The Autocar* in June 1948 on the £748 V8 Pilot.

WHO LOVED IT?

The Pilot was adored by demob spivs, and its whole image was quite 'gangster', with its standard black, dark green or beige paintwork, big headlights and burly-looking profile. It could seat a 'mob' of six on two bench seats. At the time, Ford's British reputation was as a manufacturer of extremely basic economy cars, so the Pilot hardly had a prestige image. That was probably why only 22,255 found buyers in four short years, despite its certain status as a motoring bargain.

This Pilot is just about to drive over 3in metal spikes at 60mph at Lulsgate Aerodrome, Bristol, to see if Goodyear's Lifeguard Safety Tube tyres lived up to their name.

Jowett Javelin, 1947

A world-beating car ... from Bradford? Well, yes, actually. When first revealed in a 'sneak' public preview at the British motor industry's Golden Jubilee Parade in London in 1946, the Javelin turned the company's reputation for coarse, flat-twin-engined runabouts on its head.

During the Second World War Jowett had plenty of Ministry of Defence engineering work to sustain it. But by 1942 thoughts were turning to peacetime, and a tough but modern saloon car oozing export appeal. The company recruited sports car-mad MG designer Gerald Palmer to oversee it. It was a dream job for him because he would create the entire car from scratch – body, engine, interior, the

lot. In fact, the only parts he didn't design were the gearbox and back axle. Palmer made good roadholding, performance and space utilisation priorities, but he also wanted the car to have 'showroom appeal'.

The simple brief was for a 'six-passenger family utility', but the car ended up by far the most sophisticated family car in Britain.

It featured unitary body/chassis construction where rivals still had a separate frame. There was supple torsion-bar suspension all round, independent at the front, rack-and-pinion steering and a passenger compartment in which even those in the back sat within the wheelbase, giving excellent ride comfort.

Palmer redesigned the traditional Jowett flat-twin engine, adding two extra cylinders and enlarging it to 1,486cc, and it was mated to a four-speed gearbox.

And the whole thing was clothed in a wind-cheating, teardrop-shaped body as up to date as anything from the technically more adventurous Italy or Germany.

Because it was light, aerodynamic and high-geared, the Javelin could belt along at 80mph, with excellent acceleration, and cruise all day without getting unduly het up.

Neat details included a spare wheel that could be wound down from its hiding place under the floor.

The company took the car rallying, with designer Palmer himself helping drive the then-untried car to a class win in the 1949 Monte Carlo Rally. Shortly afterwards he was back at MG, working on the ZA Magnette and the MGA twin-cam engine, and Jowett sadly went into rapid decline.

The streamlined profile of the Javelin followed advanced German and Italian design trends, and was the epitome of modernity.

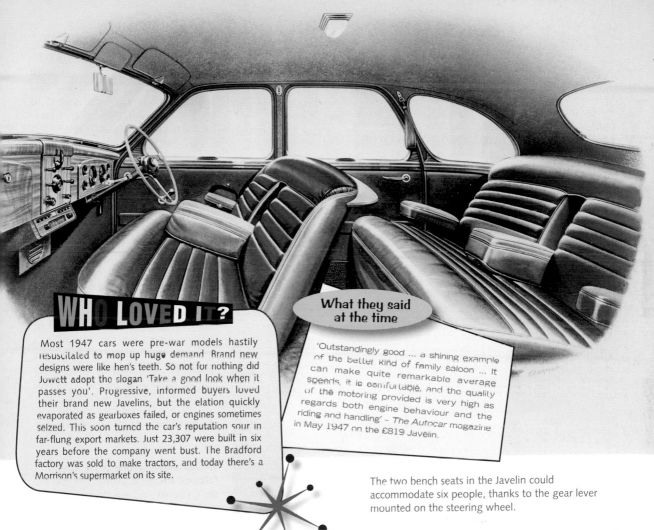

WHO LOVED IT?

Most 1947 cars were pre-war models hastily resuscitated to mop up huge demand. Brand new designs were like hen's teeth. So not for nothing did Jowett adopt the slogan 'Take a good look when it passes you'. Progressive, informed buyers loved their brand new Javelins, but the elation quickly evaporated as gearboxes failed, or engines sometimes seized. This soon turned the car's reputation sour in far-flung export markets. Just 23,307 were built in six years before the company went bust. The Bradford factory was sold to make tractors, and today there's a Morrison's supermarket on its site.

What they said at the time

'Outstandingly good ... a shining example of the better kind of family saloon ... It can make quite remarkable average speeds, it is comfortable, and the quality of the motoring provided is very high as regards both engine behaviour and the riding and handling' – *The Autocar* magazine in May 1947 on the £819 Javelin.

The two bench seats in the Javelin could accommodate six people, thanks to the gear lever mounted on the steering wheel.

11

Standard Vanguard Phase I & II, 1947

Nationalisation fever gripped Britain after the Second World War, as first the railways and then the coal industry came under state control. Car company chiefs feared they'd be next, so Standard's Sir John Black hedged his bets to secure a place in any new order: Standard would pursue a 'one model' policy to stake out its industry niche, while also making sure this car was an export-friendly, mid-sized model that could become its speciality.

To an X-framed chassis adapted from the pre-war Standard 14hp model was fitted an all-new 2,088cc four-cylinder engine with 'wet' cylinder liners to ease replacement. This robust and gutsy engine went on to power everything from Triumph TR sports cars to Ferguson tractors.

Clothing this was a streamlined, full-width body with six side windows, which looked like a contemporary full-width American sedan shrunk in the wash. In fact, the company's stylist Walter Belgrove had been ordered to hang around the American embassy in London with his crayons and sketch all the latest American cars, for inspiration.

Standard duly sent the Vanguard abroad by the boatload, sometimes in kit form for local assembly. There were estate cars, vans and pick-ups too. But its hasty development soon showed through. Prototypes had been tested only in the British Isles, and production cars had trouble in the heat, dust and terrible road conditions found outside Blighty. The engine suffered breathing and oil-pressure issues, the doors weren't sealed properly, and the chassis could barely cope with the constant light punishment of cobbles in continental cities like Brussels. The Phase I certainly lacked the legendary durability of the Plymouths and Fords the Vanguard vaguely resembled.

The Standard Vanguard

Original brochure for the Vanguard; Standard was staking out its place in the industry with this saloon, just in case it got nationalised!

Still, it offered solid performance, and each nark was rectified as it came to light. Overdrive arrived in 1950 on the Phase IA, then a bigger rear window in 1952. The Phase II of 1953 boasted more passenger and luggage space, and the first diesel engine option in any British car, but the distinctive, curved rear end was usurped by a conventional 'notchback' tail.

Of Phase Is there were 184,799, Phase IIs 81,074. The Phase III of 1956 was completely different, with unitary construction and Italian styling, but it still struggled against rivals with better reputations.

The Phase II Vanguard swapped its beetle-back shape for a conventional boot, and was also available as Britain's first diesel-powered car.

What they said at the time

'In accelerating from low speed, pinking occurs on the present British Pool petrol, but on fuel of higher octane value available elsewhere this would no doubt disappear. As a whole it is a smooth and quiet running engine' – *The Autocar* magazine in July 1947 on the £543 Vanguard.

A close-up of the original Vanguard's radiator grille highlights the bold chromework copied from American sedans of the time.

WHO LOVED IT?

This was a bold, if flawed, attempt to make a world-class British saloon car, and the simplicity of its mechanical package – as much as its daring styling – gave it broad appeal. Standard also did quite well with big fleet orders, supplying large batches of Vanguards as staff cars to the armed forces, the RAF in particular, and as company cars to big companies.

Citroën 'Traction Avant', 1948

Just like its domestic rival Renault, France's Citroën had operated a satellite assembly plant in Slough, Berkshire since the 1920s, and here the much-loved Traction Avant, or 'Front-Wheel Drive', was assembled for British and Commonwealth customers with locally-sourced parts like wheels, radiators, seats, bumpers and instruments.

This astonishing car was launched back in 1934, and the effort of bringing it to market virtually bankrupted Citroën because it was jam-packed with new technology. It was rushed into production, so the early ones had teething troubles, but once Michelin had taken over the company, the problems were quickly fixed, and the Traction Avant went on to be extremely successful and long-lived, sticking around in the Citroën catalogue until 1957.

Aside from its front-driven wheels – very unusual then for a mass-production car, and a guarantor of excellent roadholding – it also featured chassis-less monocoque construction, the gearbox in front of the engine for a low centre of gravity, all-round independent suspension, and yet also possessed lines that were rakish, stylish and considerably lower than most mainstream saloons. The great W.O. Bentley owned one for years, and loved it.

In the UK, post-war, you could have the lively 1,911cc overhead-camshaft four-cylinder in either the compact Light 15 or the roomier, longer Big 15, with both derivatives gaining a more capacious and prominent boot to take an internal spare wheel from 1952. But the model that the whole nation knew

WHO LOVED IT?

If you were a driver of discernment, and enjoyed a car that could be thrown around with gusto, this Citroën was for you. All the Slough-built cars were tailored to British tastes, with a 12-volt electric system (instead of 6), leather upholstery, wooden dashboards and a wider choice of colours than the standard black seen on just about every French-made Traction Avant.

This Citroën was one of very few front-wheel-drive cars available at the time, and was so superb to drive that the great W.O. Bentley was an enthusiastic owner.

well from its appearance in BBC TV's hugely popular adaptation of Georges Simenon's *Maigret* was the Big Six, an opulent 'Traction' with a 2.9-litre straight-six engine. This particular model also helped usher in the high-tech era of the DS, as it introduced Citroën's first hydro-pneumatic, self-levelling suspension system in 1954. That certainly wouldn't be the car to go for if you wanted low running costs, though.

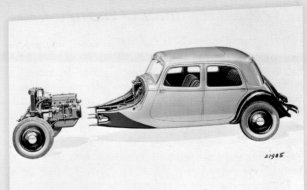

This shows how the front-wheel drive 'powerpack' enabled the rest of the car to be focused solely on passenger space.

What they said at the time

'Roll on corners may occur with this car in a strictly geometrical sense, but it is so slight that neither driver nor passengers are ever really conscious of it. The same is true of the nose-dipping during hard braking. The really pleasant cruising speed is 50mph' – *The Motor* magazine in March 1951 on the £812 Citroën Light Fifteen.

Running boards weren't required because the delightfully styled Citroën was low-slung anyway.

Ford Anglia & Popular, 1948

These little Fords were at the bottom of the pile when it came to comfort, sophistication and performance. On the other hand, their super low prices offered many people their first chance of a brand new car. Narrow and upright, everyone called them the 'sit up and beg' Fords.

The Anglia could trace its roots back directly to the Model Y of 1932, the first Ford designed (in Detroit) specially for the British market. So the gutless, side-valve, four-cylinder engine of 933cc was well behind the times when the 1948 Anglia was launched with a more streamlined frontage and a very slightly updated interior.

As there were leaf springs both front and back, the ride was jarring, and the antediluvian mechanical brakes were on the worrying side of adequate. As acceleration was pitiful and top speed a mere 57mph, the three-speed gearbox wasn't a handicap. Most owners were much more focused on its 36mpg fuel economy.

You might have thought such an old-fashioned vehicle would have had its days numbered in the post-war era. But in 1953, as the much more modern 100E models came on stream (see page 84), Ford decided to give the car a new lease of life.

The name was changed to Popular, and there was a larger 1,172cc engine, but every possible frill was removed, and that included the chrome on the bumpers, one of the windscreen wipers and the indicators. The headlamps were reduced in size and there was no heater.

Rather than being a bar to its popularity, the rock-bottom price – it was consistently the cheapest four-wheeled passenger car you could buy new – put this car in constant demand, and over 150,000 were sold right up to 1959.

American custom-car fans of the 1960s and '70s had the Model T and Model A on which to work their magic, but the Anglia and 'Pop' were Britain's equivalent.

It might have been antediluvian but the bargain-basement Popular, with side valves and leaf springs, was on sale until 1959.

WHO LOVED IT?

If you were a bit short of cash but wanted a new car then this was the one for you. It really flourished at a time when there was a still nationwide scarcity of second-hand cars, and much as it was uncomfortable and super-basic, it was tough as old boots. Worn-out examples were often used to build kit cars, and later, in the 1960s and '70s, the 'Pop' formed the basis of many a hot rod.

What they said at the time

'The clutch has a firmness of grip which can induce judder if the driver is clumsy. The suspension sometimes causes a considerable amount of vertical movement, especially during quick negotiation of rough roads. Whatever it might lack in refinement, the Anglia is a car in big demand' – *The Motor* magazine in 1950 on the £309 Ford Anglia.

If you worked as a rep for the Scott-Bathgate confectionery company, you got one of these Anglias for the sweet shop rounds on your sales patch.

Hillman Minx Phase III–VIII, 1948

The Minx lineage was just as venerable as the Ford Anglia one on the previous pages, with the first of these no-nonsense economy cars also dating back to 1932 and relying on rather asthmatic side-valve engines. The Minx was conceived to be robust and reliable, but the Rootes Group who made it was almost never at the cutting edge when it came to mechanical innovation. What they were concerned with was sales appeal, and the Minx always had plenty of surface features that Hillman salesmen could wax lyrical over.

And so it was with the Phase III model unveiled in 1948. The full-width styling had a quasi-American feel to it, thanks to input from design consultants at New York's Loewy Studios, while the bench front seat and column gear change meant that you could squeeze in six people.

This, however, was asking a lot of the faithful 1,185cc side-valve engine, although the steering was light and the independent front suspension gave decent ride quality. The motor was upped in capacity to 1,265cc for the Phase IV, but only

with the VIII in 1954 did the Minx get a modern, overhead-valve power unit of 1,390cc. Top speed leapt from 56 to 77mph, but the real attraction was that the unit allowed the car to achieve higher cruising speeds and lower engine revs, so it was much more pleasant to drive. A front anti-roll bar now meant the Minx coped with the engine's more athletic urge, but ride comfort suffered a little.

Another aspect that cheered Hillman dealers was the wide choice of bodies, with the Minx available as saloon and estate, a convertible or a hardtop Coupé optimistically called the Californian, and a basic, short-wheelbase utility estate called the Husky. In 1956, too, you could opt for a styling package called the 'Gay Look', which meant jazzy two-tone paintwork, extra chrome trim, and not so much as a snigger about the title in those innocent times.

By the time this cosmetically enhanced Phase VIII model arrived the Minx finally offered the overhead-valve engine it so badly needed.

The racy roofline, pillar-less side windows and snug rear quarters identify this as the Minx Californian Hardtop.

WHO LOVED IT?

The Minx was one for Mr Sensible, being smart and up to date as far as the neighbours were concerned, yet technically simple for everyday use and ease/cheapness of maintenance. It was also, oddly, popular in Japan, where the car was licence-built by Isuzu and became a foundation stone of the country's entire motor industry. They literally learnt to make cars by building this Minx; few of the Japanese public could afford one, so most became taxis in and around Tokyo.

What they said at the time

'The latest Minx impressed us as being a very well-mannered car from every angle, and there is no doubt the new engine with its improved performance and noticeably sweeter and quieter running, has made this Mk IV edition an outstandingly good car in its class' – *The Motor* magazine in 1950 on the £505 Minx Mk IV.

The Minx estate, photographed in 1953, was a boxy number, which wasn't surprising because the Commer Cob delivery van shared the same basic body.

Humber Hawk Mk III–VI, 1948

This large saloon from the upmarket division of the Rootes Group offered a similar looking take on contemporary American styling to its smaller Hillman Minx stablemate. The Hawk, with its modern curved windscreen and plastic dashboard, was also built in Coventry, England's bustling motor city answer to Detroit.

Unfortunately, it likewise ran an old-fashioned side-valve engine – such a limited-performance unit was okay in the Minx, and also in the large and stately 4-litre Humber Super Snipe. But in the Hawk the result was severely limited acceleration, and a bit too much noise and vibration when pressed hard. Even when the Mk III's 1.9-litre, four-cylinder power unit was boosted to 2.2 litres in 1952 for the Mk IV, with improved steering and higher gearing, it was still quite wearing to do 70mph for any length of time.

Belatedly, Rootes did fit an overhead-valve engine in the Mk VI in 1954. Now the top speed was well over 80mph, cruising was enjoyable at 70mph (even more so with the optional overdrive), and the car could still manage 27mpg. At the same time, the '54 Hawk gained a more elegant look with extended rear wings. In this respect, it came into line with the Super Snipe introduced two years before, which itself used a basic Hawk body with a longer bonnet to accommodate the big, powerful 4.1-litre, straight-six engine it shared with Commer trucks.

All these big Humbers retained a robust separate chassis frame under their modern-looking bodies and so, despite having independent front suspension, they were lumbering cars that didn't invite spirited cornering. What they did have was plenty of space for passengers, high ground clearance, and a good deal of regal presence.

A Humber Hawk takes a rest outside Buckingham Palace as a coach full of tourists thunders past, around 1953.

Not sure if either of the claims at the head of this Hawk brochure from 1952 ring true, but it was certainly a comfy conveyance.

What they said at the time

'The driver is attracted initially by a good driving position with a large thin-rimmed wheel which he sits well above, giving him at once a sense of command, and with vision that is notably assisted by a wide windscreen' – *The Autocar* magazine in 1951 on the £799 Hawk.

The Mk IV Hawk of 1950 featured a lower bonnet line and hefty wraparound bumpers with prominent overriders.

Neat details of the 1950 Mk IV, although you still had to fork out extra to get yourself that fancy pushbutton radio set.

WHO LOVED IT?

Thanks to extensive use as rugged army staff cars during the Second World War – including General Montgomery's famous 'Old Faithful' – there was huge respect and affection for the big Humbers. Many buyers felt a real bond with the cars, and were prepared to overlook their dated specifications. Bigger models, including Super Snipe, Pullman and Imperial, were also favourites with Whitehall ministries and other government bodies, giving Humber a place at the heart of the British establishment.

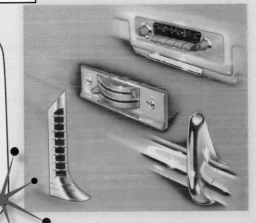

Land Rover Series I, 1948

The Land Rover Defender still on sale in the second decade of the twenty-first century is the direct descendent of this very first Landie, a go-anywhere vehicle the like of which no one had known before back in 1948.

Rover's four-wheel drive, tractor/pick-up hybrid was aimed at farmers and made from war-surplus materials, principally aircraft-grade aluminium, to get around steel shortages. Willys Jeep axles and body frame had been used as templates during the design process, but Maurice Wilks, the Rover director whose baby it was, decreed: 'It must be along the lines of the Willys Jeep but much more versatile, more useful as a power source, be able to do everything.'

The Land Rover got the go-ahead for manufacture in September 1947 – as a stopgap product while the company grappled with steel supply issues to restart car making. The only Jeep connection was its identical 80in wheelbase, and most components came from the old Rover 60 saloon, including the 1,595cc four-cylinder engine and axles. The only bespoke item required was a 4×4 power transfer case, and the bodywork was simplified so Rover's production-line workers could form the panels using low-cost jigs and hand tools.

It was launched at the Amsterdam motor show in January 1948 at a mere £450, albeit to an extremely basic specification. When it went on sale in July that year, there was just one paint colour, Avro green (more war surplus) and the standard spec now included a spare wheel and a rudimentary canvas hood.

WHO LOVED IT?

Rover planned to sell just fifty Land Rovers a week as a sideline, eventually concentrating again on building Rover cars. But within a year, demand for this brilliant vehicle was so strong that henceforth Land Rover became the profitable bedrock of Rover's business.

The Land Rover was a brilliant four-wheel-drive hybrid of pick-up and tractor that unleashed massive rural demand.

With a 50bhp engine and a healthy 80lb ft of torque at 2,000rpm, the Land Rover bounded nimbly up and down slippery hills. Excellent wheel articulation thanks to tough leaf-spring suspension and athletic approach/departure angles of 45/35° were real assets.

Four-wheel drive was permanent and, with no central differential and a freewheel in the front drive to reduce tyre scrub, slightly uncoordinated. In 1950, an ingenious dogleg clutch fixed that, permitting selectable two- or four-wheel drive; the definitive Land Rover 'system' had arrived.

Pulling power counted, not acceleration, so the tardy 0–40mph time of 18 seconds was irrelevant, and it offered 24mpg, something farmers really approved of.

What they said at the time

'The Land Rover Station Wagon is an outstanding car that can be driven almost anywhere. The vehicle is ideally suited to towing a caravan or a horsebox, and is completely free of unnecessary frills. It is a first-rate machine' – *The Autocar* magazine in March 1955 on the £893 short-wheelbase Station Wagon.

This 80in Station Wagon made the Land Rover slightly more car-like, and could seat eight in bouncy discomfort.

Morris Minor, 1948

The Morris Minor was one economy car that drove, steered and handled outstandingly yet was still roomy, affordable and economical. The engineer Alec Issigonis envisioned the Minor during the Second World War, seeing no reason such a small car couldn't drive and handle well. So he positioned the engine further forward than normal for a better centre of gravity, specified rack-and-pinion steering and designed torsion-bar independent front suspension, which gave the Minor a less jarring ride than rivals (Morris accountants vetoed his plan for the system at the back so he was stuck with an old-fashioned live axle located by leaf springs with lever arm dampers).

The two-door bodywork design, meanwhile, was virtually signed off in 1947 when Issigonis suddenly decided the car was too narrow. He halted all development work while he sawed a prototype in half from nose to tail to insert 4in more width. That's why the crest of the car's roof running from front to back is completely flat.

One throwback to older Morris cars was the 918cc side-valve, four-

A very early Morris Minor, with lights set low beside the radiator grille, photographed in Monaco in 1949.

The Traveller estate, introduced in 1953, was a masterpiece of craftsmanship, as the wooden frame supported the steel panels.

cylinder, 27.5bhp engine, which meant the Minor huffed and puffed to its maximum speed of just 60mph.

Most of these first cars, the Minor MM-type saloons and convertibles, were exported, so British demand was pent-up for them. In 1950 the headlamps were moved from the grille to high up on the front wings, to satisfy American lighting rules. Ironically, this was just when transatlantic sales collapsed because Americans found it gutless and flimsy.

In 1950, too, a four-door saloon was announced, the legendary two-door Traveller estate following in 1953, by which time the car had gained the 803cc overhead-valve engine from Morris's new British Motor Corporation stablemate, the Austin A30. In 1956 the Minor's divided windscreen was replaced by a one-piece item, and its engine size boosted to 948cc to become the Morris Minor 1000.

The dextrous Issigonis designed the Traveller's 'timbered' back end himself, and the eighty wood, metal and glass parts fitted together with Lego-like precision. This helps make Minors simple to restore, one factor behind their high survival rate, with 60,000 still extant in the UK alone.

WHO LOVED IT?

This car so suited its native land that, in 1960, it became the first British car to sell a million examples. The last one was made as late as 1971, by which time 1,583,619 Minors had found buyers. Why so popular? Minors were sedate performers but were full of character, very frugal, had excellent ride and beautifully light, responsive steering. Their features soon became comforting touchstones of everyday motoring, such as the flashing green light on the end of the indicator stalk, the central speedo, and the farty exhaust noise when changing gear.

This picture was actually taken in February 1961, but the majority of the first million Minors were sold in the 1950s.

MORRIS MINOR 1.000.000

Life on the Road in 1950s Britain

By 1950, British drivers had endured five years of post-war motoring gloom and deprivation. The continuing petrol rationing and tight restrictions on sales of new and second-hand cars were frustrating enough, but the country's roads were still in a dismal state after the widespread damage they'd sustained during five years of war.

Throughout the 1940s patch repairs and temporary fixes were the norm, as local councils struggled to tackle the severe pounding the road network had received from heavy military trucks and tanks. Work by donkey-jacketed gangs was hampered further by the extremely severe winter of 1947. Getting around was made doubly difficult because the reinstatement of directional signs taken down

in 1940 – as a precaution against an invasion – was so sporadic … and they often reappeared at the wrong junctions!

The country was on its uppers. The government was committed to repaying its wartime debts and driving ahead with currency-earning exports, while simultaneously improving the lot of the ordinary citizen, ground down by war, with initiatives like nationalisation and the new National Health Service. Improving the road network for driver enjoyment and convenience was a relatively low priority.

Nonetheless, in 1946, Whitehall indicated that new roads were an important factor. It issued a 'Grand Plan' that outlined various schemes that could go ahead 'once essential maintenance and repairs of existing highways

Below left: Driving on British roads in the early 1950s, such as in this Ford Prefect, was an unalloyed pleasure, with restrictions few and traffic less than a sixth of today's volume.

Below centre: Bad weather often stymied 1940s and '50s drivers; this is the morning of 1 January 1951 when a mini-blizzard hit London, here Ludgate Circus – note the radiator muffler on the truck's grille.

Below right: This is the Lygon Arms Hotel in Broadway, Worcestershire in about 1952, with guest parking not a problem. Left to right, they are Vanguard, Minx, Six-Eighty, Morris Eight Series E, Consul and another Vanguard.

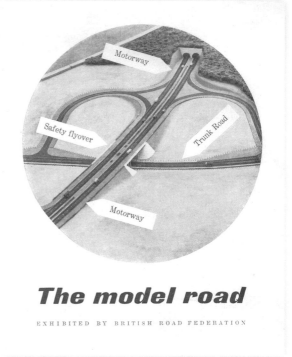

The model road

EXHIBITED BY BRITISH ROAD FEDERATION

Above: Two cars pass each other on the Menai suspension bridge in the mid 1950s, a Standard Vanguard on the left and an Austin A35 heading towards the camera.

Above right: Front cover of the British Road Federation's persuasive 1952 brochure helping its campaign for a proper motorway network.

are completed'. The most concrete plan was for a new trunk road that linked Swansea, Cardiff and Newport, swept across the Severn estuary and then went on up to the West Midlands, but there was much talk around a new series of 'Motor Roads' – the first inkling of a motorway network – resembling the M5, M6, M25 and M42 that would eventually materialise, as well as bringing

A fleet of shiny new AA rescue vehicles line up ready for action just prior to the opening of the M1 in 1959.

the A1 up to motorway standards. That year, though, the only major project to get started was the approach roads to the Dartford Tunnel, and even that work ground to a halt soon after under tight financial restrictions.

Indeed, it wasn't until 1953 – seven years later – that a proper road-building programme was announced. Construction was already underway on the A20 Ashford bypass in Kent, the Maidenhead bypass in Berkshire (now the M4), the A4 Cromwell Road extension in west London and the restarted Dartford Tunnel. Now detailed plans were laid for the Preston and Lancaster bypasses in Lancashire (today part of the M6), the Heads of the Valleys road in South Wales (today's A465), a Port Talbot bypass (A48) and Scotland's Ross spur road (M50).

Two years later, in 1955, flesh was put on these bones as a spending programme of £212m was announced along with additions to the scope of the venture. This included turning the A74 between Carlisle and Glasgow into a dual-carriageway, adding bypasses and two-lane sections to winding and narrow parts of the A1, a green light for the Forth Road Bridge and, most significantly of all, giving the go-ahead to the first purpose-built motorway, the M1 between Crick and Coventry.

In fact, the first motorway section to open would be an upgrade of the long-proposed Preston bypass (today's M6); construction began in 1956 and the 8.5-mile stretch saw its first traffic in November 1958.

Motorways themselves would really be a feature of 1960s driving, but lobbying for them stretched right back to 1948. That was the year the British Road Federation, a pressure group of 112 organisations with interests in motoring, road haulage and highway construction,

Above: The introduction of affordable mass-produced caravans, like this lightweight Sprite Ariel hitched up to an Austin A30 in 1958, led to a boom in motoring holidays.

Right: Mobile phones were a sci-fi movie pipe dream, and the AA had to make clever use of landlines linking up their phone boxes.

Opposite: Cars in the 1950s routinely suffered major mechanical failures, so you would have been glad to see this Ford Thames recovery truck arrive from Birmingham's Bristol Street Motors to tow you home.

began its vociferous 'The Case For Motorways' campaign under the slogan of 'Roads to fit the traffic, not traffic to fit the road'. By 1952, it was hawking a working model around shows and exhibitions, with electrically powered toy cars travelling along a miniature motorway system, to show how vehicles would never need to cut across one another or encounter any pedestrians, so reducing accidents. It claimed motorway building was actually cheaper than adapting existing roads, and that the British economy would see efficiency savings of £15m a year once the government's 1,000-mile motorway network was completed. It even trumpeted the aesthetic improvements motorways would usher in: 'With two carriageways, with an anti-dazzle hedge in between, the motorway threads its way gracefully across the countryside. Along it there are no unsightly commercial or building developments which disfigure so many of our roads today. A motorway is planned as a whole to "fit in" to the landscape.'

AA patrols – radio-linked from 1949 – travelled with their Land Rovers stacked with tools, and many repairs could be easily carried out at the roadside, such as on this Hillman Minx.

During the 1940s, there was almost no growth in traffic. In 1950, there were 3,870,000 licensed vehicles running around, of which 1,979,000 were cars, and those figures were pretty close to the stats of 1939. The 1950s, though, would see a near doubling of volume. By 1955 there were 5,822,000 licensed vehicles, 3,109,000 of them cars, and by 1959 the total had ballooned to 7,809,000 vehicles, including 4,416,000 cars. So no wonder the cries grew louder across the land for more bypasses, as towns were gridlocked by the traffic burden.

There was a speed limit of 30mph in built-up areas with street lighting, although this was only made permanent in 1956 after having been renewed yearly on a temporary basis since 1935. In 1957, the blanket maximum speed for lorries and other goods vehicles was raised from 20 to 30mph. Apart from that, car drivers could drive as fast as they liked. And this, among others things, made British roads – which in the mid 1950s were the busiest and most crowded on earth – particularly dangerous.

A Jaguar Mk VII driven by Minister of Transport A.T. Lennox-Boyd 'cuts' the ribbon at the opening of the Motor Industry Research Association proving ground at Nuneaton, Warwickshire on 21 May 1954; the establishment did much to improve the safety and reliability of new cars.

The all-time record for annual road deaths was set in 1941, in the middle of the blacked-out war, at a shocking 9,169, so the 1950 total of 5,012, along with 196,000 recorded injuries, would seem to have been a vast improvement. Yet by 1960 the figures had shot up: 6,970 people were killed and 341,000 injured.

One initiative to reduce this carnage had already been set in motion in 1947, when a scheme to embed cat's eyes in Britain's rural roads went nationwide. They had been undergoing trials since 1937, but their life-saving possibilities were undeniable. The initiative to install them everywhere was taken by Junior Transport Minister (and future British Prime Minister) James Callaghan, who was also firmly behind another move to improve safety: the zebra crossing.

It was actually a refinement of the standardised pedestrian road crossing introduced in 1934. That had had two rows of bright metal studs traversing the road between which pedestrians could cross, with a black-and-white striped pole at each side, topped with an orange

glass globe (later painted metal) and known as a Belisha Beacon after the then Transport Minister Leslie Hore-Belisha.

Callaghan's version now had broad black and white alternating stripes painted across the dark tarmac, and in 1952 the Belisha Beacons began to be fitted with a flashing bulb inside an orange plastic globe.

In 1954 the fourth edition of *The Highway Code* was published, the first in full colour, and along with posters issued by the Royal Society for the Prevention of Accidents (RoSPA), the exhortations not to drive while drunk were louder than ever, although breathalysers weren't introduced until 1967. Other 1950s road-safety campaigns were tilted at children, such as RoSPA's 1952 Teddy Club aimed at educating the under-sixes, and the character of Tufty Fluffytail in a series of children's stories, whose own later Tufty Club was a totem of every 1960s British childhood. For grown-ups wanting to protect themselves through better driving, 1956 saw the launch of the Institute of Advanced Motorists; by 1960 it could boast 20,000 members, and its campaigning work continues to this very day.

Some things vanished from our roads during the 1950s, such as London's trams. Others popped up

for the first time, like the country's first ever motel, at Newingreen, between Dover and Folkestone, Kent; the first Motorail car train service between London King's Cross and Perth in 1955 (return fare £15 for car and overnight sleeping driver); and the first parking meters in 1958, in London's Grosvenor Square, which required 6d (2.5p) for an hour's stay.

Above left: A major altercation between a Vauxhall and a Wolseley in the early 1950s, when British road deaths and injuries were rising. You can just see graffiti reading 'Smash the Tories' on the wall behind!

Above centre: Renault was among the first to crash-test its cars to improve occupant safety; here a speeding truck is about to see how a Dauphine stands up to a front three-quarters shunt in 1955.

Above right: The British roadscape was rapidly changing with, for example, trams running for the last time on London's streets in 1952.

Morris Oxford MO, 1948

This one looks just like a Morris Minor but on a slightly bigger all-round scale, and for that reason today it's something of a forgotten car. However, it was launched alongside the Minor at the 1948 Earl's Court Motor Show, where Morris gave it just as much importance as the smaller car. And the fact that it went on to achieve over 160,000 sales in a little over five years is a good measure of its success.

Like a lot of larger British saloons of the late 1940s and early '50s, the Oxford was saddled with a gutless side-valve engine, of 1,476cc. It was reasonably smooth but the car was anything but vivid in the performance department, and was hard work on hills. This was a real shame because the rest of its technical spec, overseen by engineer Alec Issigonis, was excellent: unitary construction, rack-and-pinion steering, hydraulic brakes, torsion-bar front suspension – its road manners were good and it could cope manfully with rough road surfaces.

Actually, you could have an Oxford-type car with an overhead-camshaft engine. This was the Oxford-based Wolseley Four-Fifty, which boasted a prominent tradi-tional radiator grille and a fine level of interior appointment including individual front seats instead of the Oxford's bench, but Wolseley's own engine offered only slightly better acceleration and top speed, and needed a lot more maintenance.

Oxford choice extended to a wood-framed Traveller estate car in 1952, and van and pick-up editions were also on offer. Good vehicles, the lot of them, but definitely from a pre-motorway era when eager and sustained performance wasn't seen as important by long-established car manufacturers.

What they said at the time

'The Oxford is entirely up to date in design, having integral chassis-less construction and independent front suspension by torsion bars. One soon feels that it is a robust, go-anywhere sort of a car. It is not too big for the average private garage and is handy in narrow lanes' – *The Autocar* magazine in 1951 on the £546 Oxford.

Morris Oxfords, and a few Minors, passing the quality checklist at the end of the Cowley production line.

An Oxford made a dependable, if not particularly swift, car to go holidaying in. This one is parked in picturesque Hospenthal, Andermatt, Switzerland in the mid 1950s.

WHO LOVED IT?

A good, solid middle-class saloon, strong on space. This was a familiar sight on Britain's suburban roads throughout the 1950s, but it wouldn't have been the first choice for any driver undertaking regular, long-distance trips. Nevertheless, Oxfords did fairly well on the export front in territories where endurance rather than speed mattered. In that vein, it was built and sold commercially in India as the Hindustan 14.

No robots in sight as an Oxford body, already lead-loaded to ensure smooth lines, enters the assembly process under watchful human eyes.

Vauxhall Wyvern & Velox, 1948

Vauxhall had broken significant new ground in 1937 with its H-type 12hp range. It was the first British car based around integral monocoque construction, which got rid of the need for a separate chassis frame. This means Vauxhall was still some way ahead of many rivals in 1948, when it used the chassis-less centre section of the H-type as the basis for its new post-war range.

The junior member of the duo was the Wyvern, with a 1,442cc four-cylinder motor, while the externally near-identical – apart from bumper overriders and cream-painted wheels – Velox sported a 2,275cc straight-six. They were chalk and cheese: the Wyvern was frugal but slow, with 60mph a strain, while the Velox was uncommonly rapid because of its light weight relative to competitors, albeit a bit unnerving on twisty roads thanks to its short wheelbase, thin tyres and tall stance. But both were reasonably comfortable with their independent coil-spring front suspension, and very robust. Thanks to Vauxhall's ownership by America's General Motors, the cars found ready markets abroad, and a version was manufactured in Australia with several modifications to suit local tastes. If there was a downside then it was rust – both cars were badly prone to the dreaded tin-worm, and soon gained a notorious reputation for it.

The powerful Velox is easily distinguished from its lowly Wyvern brother by its cream-painted wheels.

You could easily tell that the centre section of the car had pre-war origins, with a modernised front end and an extended boot. They were stopgaps while Vauxhall got its factory car-focused again after spending years manufacturing tanks for the war effort. Interestingly, the Velox was the stronger seller, and this was perhaps one reason why Vauxhall decided to avoid small cars, which pulled in lower profits, until it launched the Viva of 1963.

The posing model has her work cut out trying to make the workaday Vauxhall Wyvern look smart.

WHO LOVED IT?

The Velox had real appeal as a powerful and dependable saloon with very little to worry the owner (rust patches apart). The sluggish Wyvern was perhaps a less attractive prospect, but then it could manage an easy 35mpg, and so still made plenty of sense.

GMJ 401

Wolseley Six-Eighty, 1948

Wolseley had been supplying British police forces with patrol cars since well before the war, and this all-new Six-Eighty quickly became a familiar sight with a uniformed driver at the wheel. They liked its excellent power-to-weight ratio, big drum brakes and the powerful, 72bhp, six-cylinder engine that made this an 85mph car.

This was the undisputed flagship model of the Nuffield Organisation's line-up of Morris, MG, Riley and Wolseley cars. It shared its body with the Morris Six and used the same Wolseley 2.2-litre overhead-camshaft engine, only in the Six-Eighty it had an extra 6bhp. Indeed both these cars used the structure of the Morris Oxford/Wolseley Four-Fifty but with a bonnet elongated by 7in to accommodate the bigger power unit (the wheelbase was 13in longer in total). The tall radiator grille and twin spotlights imparted power and luxury, and indeed the cabin was pretty sumptuous, with leather-upholstered seats, wooden dashboard and a heater as standard equipment.

It was quick in a straight line, but the vague steering and heavy nose, weighed down by the engine, meant high-speed manoeuvring was not a virtue. An engine design fault meant exhaust valves often burnt out after just 10,000 miles, and there was no temperature gauge. Police mechanics dealt stoically with the weak valves and guides, and all the absurd amount of greasing and oiling demanded by the suspension, while drivers simply had to be skilled and physically fit to cope with the steering.

Wolseley supplied them in a heavy-duty specification to the Metropolitan Police, with beefier anti-roll bars and electrical systems. Wireless area cars, for responding to 999 calls, sported a roof-mounted radio aerial and a chrome Winkworth gong in place of one front fog light; Motor Traffic Patrol cars, in addition, gained two Tannoy loudhailers on the roof, wider tyres, and illuminated 'POLICE' signs. Both had Pye radio transmitter/receiver units in the boot.

The Six-Eighty was a powerful car and quite rapid in a straight line, although not too well set up for spirited cornering.

WHO LOVED IT?

The Six-Eighty was actually a mixed blessing for police drivers, because once criminals started using stolen Jags as getaway cars, the dynamic limit of these Wolseleys, which were always a handful to control, was exposed. Nonetheless, the car was still in service with the fuzz as late as 1961, seven years after it finished manufacture. Just shy of 25,000 were made in total, those not used for crime-fighting providing luxury transport for many a doctor, bank manager or businessman.

When Six-Eightys' working days were over, some of them were pressed into action as practice pursuit cars at the Metropolitan Police Training School in Hendon, north London.

... Which means, presumably, that her handsome tennis partner was probably a copper, perhaps hinted at by the always-on-duty ginger beer, and rippling thigh.

Sunbeam-Talbot 90, 1948

In the hands of Finnish drivers Per Malling and Gunnar Fadum, the Sunbeam-Talbot 90 gained worldwide attention in 1955, when their car won the Monte Carlo Rally, and even achieved it with a broken fan belt in the final stages of this gruelling event. It was the sort of sporting victory that did wonders for the marque's credibility as the sporting division among the mundane brands of the Rootes Group.

The car had first appeared in mid 1948, and the omens for success did not look great. Aside from the streamlined bodywork and the 64bhp, 2-litre Humber Hawk engine converted from side- to overhead-value configuration, there were old-fashioned leaf springs back and front on the separate chassis, and a contemporarily trendy column gear change that sat oddly with individual front seats. A short-lived companion model, the 80, had a lightly fettled Hillman Minx engine and was a meek performer, albeit a reliable one.

However, in 1950, the car was given a remarkable transformation to Mk II status, with a beefed-up chassis frame and independent front suspension, a bigger 70bhp 2.2-litre motor, and a new frontage with raised headlights. And two years later, bigger, better brakes arrived on the 77bhp Mk IIA, although the sleek spats over the rear wheels were axed to make sure they could keep their cool.

Many of the improvements that transformed the car into a decent little sports saloon – it was vastly better to drive than before – were derived directly from its wide campaigning on rallies around Europe, in the hands of drivers including a young Stirling Moss, Sheila Van Damm and Tommy Wisdom. There was even a glamorous two-seater roadster version, the simply titled Sunbeam Alpine, whose very name celebrated the cars' success on punishing events, in addition to a rare and elegant four-seater drophead Coupé.

Meanwhile, in the showrooms, the car lingered until 1957, for the final three years known just as the 80bhp Sunbeam Mk III with various upgrades including optional overdrive, and a Leicester Sunbeam dealer's conversion to a floor-mounted gear change, in which form this attractive car reached its pinnacle of desirability.

'A most notable example of modern streamlining', says the caption to this image of the sporty Sunbeam-Talbot.

The Sunbeam-Talbot team pictured after finishing the 1949 International Alpine Rally, for which they scooped the Foreign Manufacturers' Team prize.

WHO LOVED IT?

The rallying Sunbeams, with excellent showings in such greats as the Alpine, Tulip, RAC and, of course, Monte Carlo rallies made this quite a desirable sports saloon throughout the early 1950s in a price bracket below a Jaguar's. The image was enhanced by handsome styling that continued to look good no matter how much chrome embellishment was attached to it by Rootes.

A speeding Mk II version of the Sunbeam-Talbot 90 in 1951, with the headlight height now significantly increased.

Bond Minicar, 1949

Aeronautical engineer Lawrence Bond spent the Second World War putting his skills and ingenuity to good use at the Blackburn Aircraft Company, but afterwards he decided to tackle a transport project of his own: a 'short radius runabout' for shopping trips and local errands – a minimal three-wheeled car, with exceptional economy and significantly more safety than a motorbike. He found a backer in a truck workshop, Sharp's Commercials, who agreed to build his Minicar at its Preston factory, and the first examples emerged in 1949.

The ingenious little machine weighed just 310lb, so light that one person could easily lift up one end of the aluminium vehicle by hand. The front wheel was driven by a single-cylinder Villiers motorcycle engine of just 122cc (hastily upgraded to 197cc) via a three-speed gearbox … with no reverse. Front suspension for the wheels and engine was courtesy of a trailing link system while at the back the wheels were simply mounted on the stressed skin body structure on stub axles, with ride comfort provided by the air in the tyres!

Driver and passenger squeezed on to a tiny bench seat, with a cargo platform behind. There were no doors and weather protection was provided by a canvas hood. The windscreen was Perspex and the single wiper manually operated, while the tiny headlights were feeble and there was just one tail light.

The Minicar was all about thrift. The low purchase cost was allied to fuel consumption that gave 75mpg easily, and probably 100mpg with extreme care. Speed was not part of the deal, although a car with just the driver on board, and presumably a flat road ahead and a decent tailwind, could be wound up to 40mph.

As soon as production was underway, the Minicar underwent constant improvement, which included a rear suspension system, glass-fibre body panels, a fixed roof, hammock-style rear seats for children, a safety-glass windscreen and, eventually, a reverse gear. But changes to the basic concept had to be tackled carefully. When the wheelbase was extended in the Mk D model, the new dynamics made this Minicar prone to toppling over.

BOND MINICAR

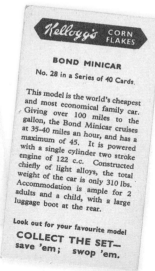

The original Bond Minicar as featured on a collector's card in a set given away with Kellogg's Corn Flakes in 1949.

The third generation Minicar sprouted these pretend front wings in an attempt to 'normalise' the quirky economy runabout.

WHO LOVED IT?

A lightweight three-wheeler was classified as a tricycle, and so levels of road tax and insurance were little more than those for a small motorbike. Any newly married former biker therefore found it a natural progression to getting a family and a proper car, and didn't even need to take another driving test. He'd have felt entirely at home getting the raucous Minicar going – with its modified kick-start system!

What they said at the time

'The car rides with a distinctly quick, firm motion. The steering is delightfully precise and high-geared. Only the brakes are open to criticism, on the grounds that, acting on the rear wheels only, they cannot provide the quickest of crash stops even though they willingly produce the squeal of two sliding tyres' – The Motor magazine in 1950 on the £242 Minicar De Luxe 197cc.

The Minicar Mk E of 1956 with '21-year old rally driver and secretary' Valerie Johnson at the wheel.

MG TD, 1949

To resume sports car manufacture as swiftly as possible after the Second World War, MG had no option but to warm-up its pre-war fare, the TB, and crank the Abingdon production line back into life. The car it renamed, logically enough, as the TC. It had the same big 19in wire wheels, fold-flat screen, crude semi-elliptic suspension and minimalist body, slab petrol tank slung across the back like a steel backpack, and was constructed over an ash frame. The body was wider now to give more elbowroom, while synchromesh on second, third and top gear made it more pleasant to drive. Hydraulic brakes were another very worthwhile improvement.

Traditionalists absolutely loved it: it was nippy – 78mph flat-out – and fun to drive and nobody seemed to mind the heavy steering and rock-hard suspension. American GIs stationed in Britain during the Second World War got their hands on TCs. Driving these gave them ear-to-ear smiles, and many took them back home to the States, sowing the seeds for an MG export bonanza in the 1940s. American orders accounted for most of the 10,000-car production run. It offered an utterly contrasting experience to anything from Detroit: involving, exhilarating and pared-down.

The ageing TC couldn't go on indefinitely, so for 1949 MG introduced the TD: same chassis, same 1,250cc four-cylinder engine, but new independent front suspension, rack-and-pinion steering, and a roomier, very slightly more modern body with bumpers and more practical, but less snazzy,

The MG was everything a traditional roadster should be, even down to the fold-flat windscreen; it went down a storm as a US export.

WHO LOVED IT?

For many dashing young chaps of the early 1950s, the MG TD was the ultimate in exhilaration. Ultimate top speed was irrelevant, as the UK had few long, fast stretches of road, but the MG offered seat-of-the-pants enjoyment, reasonably vivacious urge, wind-in-the-hair fun and low running costs. The only problem was getting hold of one because most set sail across the Atlantic for US customers.

metal disc wheels. Still, it was faster, especially in higher compression Mk II form from 1952. The TD was a big seller, racking up 29,664 units in its four-year production run. And it had charm by the bucketload.

The final flowering of the traditional MG was the TF of 1953. By smoothing the headlamps, grille and fuel tank into the body contours, MG artfully modernised the shape. Inside there were individual front seats for the first time and a restyled dashboard. Early cars had the 1,250cc engine, from 1954 a 1,500cc unit giving 63bhp to up the verve quotient.

This is how, no doubt, most TDs were seen in the UK, with hood and sidescreens firmly in place against the British weather.

Renault 760, 1949

'Lump of butter', or rather '*la motte de beurre*' – That was this little Renault's nickname in 1947, after its rounded shape and the single standard colour of a sandy yellow, the paint being war surplus formerly used on Renault-made trucks for the occupying Nazi forces. It took Renault two years to use it all up, by when, in 1949, 300 cars a day were daily pouring out of its Billancourt works in Paris.

The car, indeed, was developed mostly in secret, and against the orders of German army chiefs, with early prototypes concealed at Louis Renault's country house (controversially, he was later tried for treason as a collaborator, and his bombed-out factory was nationalised in 1945). Inspiration for its rear-mounted engine configuration came partly from Volkswagen, but Renault's design team also calculated an economical, compact four-door family car would go down a storm in centime-pinching, post-war France.

For fiscal purposes, it was rated a four horsepower car, hence the Quatre Cheveaux or 4CV title. The 747cc engine was water-cooled and drive was via a three-speed gearbox. Steering was rack and pinion, suspension was independent all-round, and the flat floorpan meant the interior was deceptively roomy for four. Any worries about wayward rear-engined handling were offset by a puny 22bhp power output. Reaching 56mph from rest took a snail-like 38sec, with a 62mph top speed. However, a 42bhp Sport model, with four-speed gearbox, could be frightening at speed on slippery roads.

Renault could barely meet demand for the car, with 1.1m eventually being made up to 1961. It wouldn't have been competitive with the Morris Minor in Britain because of a 35 per cent import duty levied on imported cars. But Renault got round this. It sent kits of bodies, engines and gearboxes from Paris to its plant in Acton, west London, where the right-hand drive cars were then assembled by British workers who added the remaining 50 per cent (by value) of the car in the form of locally-produced interior, dashboard, tyres, electrical parts, radiator and other bolt-ons, including more luxurious trim, fittings and decor.

A 750 at Beggar's Roost as it tackles the 1953 Land's End Trial; apparently the car did eventually get to the top … with the help of a tow rope.

48

WHO LOVED IT?

It qualified as a 'British' car, for sure, but as such the government demanded that 75 per cent of output had to be exported. So most Renault 750s ended up being shipped to buyers in Canada, Australia and other dominion territories. Quite a few did sell to British drivers who didn't mind the stigma of a foreign car name, attracted by the 750's tiny running costs and spacious interior.

A stylistic makeover in 1954 with chrome-plated trim tries to give the impression that there's an engine behind that frontal 'radiator' grille.

No need for cold feet in the back; this heater vent brought warm air straight from the engine compartment to the ankles.

What they said at the time

'There is no need for "clever" driving to get the Renault away from rest briskly, for when a signal changes from red to green it readily accelerates quickly enough to draw ahead of many other vehicles. The pleasant action of the three-speed gearbox greatly helps the car' – *The Motor* magazine in 1950 on the £473 760.

1954·CB75

Rover P4 Series, 1949

Rover shocked its staid and conservative customer base with its 75, the first of the complex P4 family. The full-width styling, with definite American overtones and a central spot lamp mounted right in the middle of the radiator grille, caused consternation in comfortable suburban homes across the land.

But Rover traditionalists need not have fretted. All the solid Rover attributes were still intact with the exception of a column-mounted gear lever, and even that was back on the floor by 1954, at which point the rear wing line had been raised to provide a boot with chest freezer proportions.

The chassis was still separate, with twelve insulated rubber body mounting points for decent refinement, and the 2.1-litre straight-six with inlet-over-valve layout and an alloy cylinder head was mounted at the extreme front, leading to an understeer bias in the handling. If you didn't opt for overdrive then the engine came with a freewheel clutch, a traditional feature that pleased long-time Rover devotees.

After four years, a four-cylinder Rover 60 and a 2.6-litre 'six' Rover 90 joined the 75, with constant styling updates that gradually made the car look more stately and reinforced the 'Auntie' nickname. Throughout the 1950s and early '60s other model variations on this trio included the 80, 95, 100, 105S and 105R, and 110, all defined by their various new engines or power outputs. No matter what model, they all shared fastidious build quality and, mostly, wonderful interiors with leather upholstery, solid African walnut dashboards, West of England cloth head linings, and a weird cranked gear lever. The 105R was, in its short time on sale, the only car with a British-designed automatic transmission around – most others came from US manufacturers.

This brochure cover for the original Rover 75 gives a not particularly realistic image of the new lines that startled the middle classes.

One of the most idiosyncratic features of the all-new P4 was its 'Cyclops eye' spotlight in the grille centre, a detail that was soon deleted.

A P4 body is carefully lowered on to its chassis at Rover's Solihull plant, which had a justified reputation for quality.

WHO LOVED IT?

The shock of the new was quickly digested and these Rovers settled into being the default choice for professional people like doctors, solicitors and bank managers – pillars of British society; they were restrained, robust, comfy, refined and almost as well made as a Rolls-Royce without being anything like as flashy. The P4 lasted until 1964, and more than 130,000 were sold.

What they said at the time

'The road manners of the Rover are only unconventional in so far as they are unusually good. No attempt has been made to provide sports car performance or cornering characteristics, but when driven as a touring car, the 75 can hardly be faulted' – *The Motor* magazine in May 1952 on the £1,487 75.

Triumph Mayflower, 1949

Standard-Triumph certainly didn't concern itself too much with market research in the period leading up to the 1950s. The Mayflower was another car, following the Standard Vanguard, conceived in the head of the company's managing director, Sir John Black. His thoughts, in summary, were that rich American housewives might be tempted into a Limey shopping car if it slightly resembled an expensive limousine.

The result was one of the oddest-looking small four-seater saloons around. The upper section featured starchy 'razor-edge' lines in the style of a coach-built Rolls, and there was a tall, majestic radiator grille. But the flanks were slab sides with a straight-through wing line like a US sedan – very strange, not to say downright ugly.

The body broke new ground in being a unitary-construction design, S-T's first, but the engine was the 1.2-litre side-valve four-cylinder from the pre-war Standard 10, modernised with an aluminium cylinder head, while the three-speed all-synchromesh gearbox and back axle were shared with the Vanguard. This lot made for a slow and lifeless performance, with a top speed of about 62mph and leaden acceleration – 0–50mph took an agonising 26 seconds.

On the other hand, the car's suspension was comfortable yet robust, and the very low gearing meant you hardly had to refer to the gearbox at all. You could start off in first gear, and change into top at just 10mph. From that point of view, it might have had appeal to chic ladies about town, along with the richly appointed interior and the four upright seats, albeit the two in the back being a bit pinched because of the intrusion of the back axle. But in the US, intermediate-distance highway speeds were too much for the Mayflower, and sales there ended up being negligible. So much for the imagery of that famous conquering ship carrying pilgrims from Plymouth …

An exhibition display of the Mayflower with panels cut away to reveal the car's inner construction and design secrets.

All that's best from Britain . . .

A view of Leblon, a suburb of Rio de Janeiro

Brazil, with its mysterious tropical forests, its great Amazonian waterway, and its beautiful capital city, offers on the one hand the luxury of modern living, and on the other the excitement of the unexplored. For meeting such a variety of conditions its people have found the Triumph Mayflower the ideal car. Built by the finest engineering craftsmen, tested under the most arduous conditions, it truly represents in every detail of its design, 'all that's best from Britain.'

The Triumph Mayflower

True, the Mayflower did suffer in the US, its crucial target market, but more than 35,000 examples were sold up to 1953, which wasn't bad for what we would now call a 'premium' small car that cost at least 25 per cent more than a Morris Minor. The light steering, superb visibility and very flexible nature in town driving had their appeal. And if you 'got' the idea of the styling then the Mayflower was a car to be quite proud of.

What they said at the time

'One particular feature is the effective form of the rubber mounting, for one can crawl along at 6mph in top gear and accelerate away without a falter. This car has a nice balance of power to weight and well chosen gear ratios' – *The Autocar* magazine in 1951 on the £505 Mayflower.

Probably not the best car Britain offered, in fact, but then the Mayflower was intended as a posh shopping trolley for American housewives.

A Mayflower emerges gasping from a dust-proofing test at the Motor Industry Research Association in Nuneaton, Warwickshire.

Ford Consul, Zephyr & Zodiac Mk I, 1950

Most of the mainstream cars we've recalled up to this point have been throwbacks, one way or another, to the pre-war era. These new Fords, though, started to properly up the ante; they were packed with new technology and up-to-the-minute design. With their launch, Ford's eventual dominance of the British car market was under starter's orders.

The Consul was set to take the place of the ancient four-door Prefect while the Zephyr would replace the V8 Pilot at the top of the Ford range. But the cars were worlds apart from these relics.

They shared a brand new monocoque (unitary construction) body whose straight-through wing line and part-concealed rear wheels adopted the latest styling trends from Ford's Detroit nerve centre. The impact is a bit lost today, but the Consul and Zephyr really did look modern, and the cars were considerably lighter and more torsionally rigid than their rivals.

They were also much more agile in drivers' hands, thanks to novel MacPherson strut independent front suspension, and the all-hydraulic braking system inspired confidence.

Ford's new Consul was the most up-to-the-minute family car of its day, brand new from nose to tail.

Brand new engines were overhead-valve all round, with a lively 1.5-litre four-cylinder for the Consul launched in 1950, and a powerful 2.6-litre straight-six for the Zephyr that followed a year later. In a straight line, this could give a Jaguar some trouble, although it would always be out-classed in corners.

The duo was a success from the word go, and Ford's vast Dagenham factory struggled to cope with demand. The plant was so frantic that estate car and convertible versions (the Zephyr's had a power-operated top)

were farmed out to coachbuilders. And it took until 1954 for the flashy Zephyr Zodiac version to join the range, with its two-tone paint, whitewall tyres, spotlights and an additional 3bhp of power.

Ford's large saloon range gained an enormous image boost in 1953 when a Zephyr won the Monte Carlo Rally in the hands of Maurice Gatsonides (the man who later invented the Gatso speed camera). On public roads, meanwhile, Consuls and Zephyrs quickly became a very common sight indeed.

WHO LOVED IT?

These Fords genuinely raised the bar for the average family car, both in terms of usability and modern design. Drivers clearly liked the Zephyr's power and cruising capability because, of the roughly 100,000 built, these six-cylinder cars, including the Zodiac, accounted for very nearly half the sales. However, they weren't very well equipped to resist rust, so even by the early 1960s many were making their final journeys to the scrapyard.

This Zephyr is having its front brakes cooled down in a simple and effective way on the 1953 Monte Carlo Rally, which it won.

Jaguar Mk VII–IX, 1950

Unveiled to gasps of awe and admiration at the 1950 Earls Court London Motor Show, the Mk VII's impact was immediate and enormous. This saloon with beautiful, flowing lines and the magnificent XK six-cylinder, twin-cam engine was priced at £988 – unbelievably low. If, that is, you were able to actually have your cheque accepted. Very few people in Britain could buy one. It was export only, chasing US dollars, and within three days of its New York unveiling, Jaguar had 500 orders in the bag.

At over 16ft in length and weighing two tons with six people on board, the big new post-war Jaguar made an unlikely performance car, yet it could attain 100mph like this easily and in 1950s terms offered terrific acceleration from 0–60mph in 12 seconds. Its powerhouse, the XK engine, was a 3.4-litre straight six with twin camshafts in an all-aluminium head. The twin timing chains cut down on noise and the engine was fed by two 1.75in SU carburettors. The engine's large capacity and 'hemi' combustion chambers produced astonishing torque and 'revvability', as well as unheard-of reliability.

The handling of the car also set it apart from most other large saloons of the period: it was excellent, even on snow and ice, and large, servo-assisted drum brakes supplied exceptional stopping power.

The basic car had a long and glorious production life, the 1954 Mk VIIM coming with numerous detail changes, the 1956 Mk VIII adopting a single-piece windscreen and a revised cylinder head, and the 1958 Mk IX receiving a larger 3.8-litre engine.

The gorgeous Mk VII was Jaguar's new luxury saloon; not surprisingly, it decimated sales of Daimlers and Armstrong-Siddleys; this is the MK VIII of 1956.

Advertising on the cover of *The Motor* magazine In 1955. The link between Mk VII and Le Mans-winning D-type was real – they shared the same engine.

Plenty of styling tweaks kept the big Jags fresh; this two-tone beauty is the Mk IX, which came with an enlarged 3.8-litre engine.

WHO LOVED IT?

If you could afford it – and you didn't need silly money for one, as it was cheaper than a Daimler, Armstrong-Siddeley or Bristol – then your Mk VII would be a prized possession. You'd love to show off the richly appointed 'gentleman's club' cabin, with its walnut dashboard housing instruments that glowed purple at night, the gorgeous lines, and even the polished alloy camshaft covers and gleaming, stove-enamelled exhaust manifold under the bonnet. It was the Jag that really ignited desire for the marque in the Home Counties stockbroker belt, even If some felt the car to be a touch *nouveau riche*.

What they said at the time

'Considered from any angle, the Mk VII Jaguar is an outstanding car. It has extremely good performance, is very comfortable to drive and to ride in, is very completely equipped, has a modern yet dignified appearance, and is very good value – indeed, it is in that respect phenomenal' – *The Autocar* magazine in 1952 on the £1,693 Mk VII.

Keeping Your Car Going in 1950s Britain

The year 1950 truly was a year for celebration if you were a British driver, and 26 May that year was hailed by motoring organisations such as the AA and RAC as 'VP Day' – Victory for Petrol – when all rationing restrictions on fuel were finally lifted. For car owners, it had been an agonisingly long wait.

Petrol rationing had first been imposed by the government in September 1939, at the outset of the Second World War. Sales of branded petrol was banned, and all the 'juice' sold under these tight regulations was known as 'pool petrol' in a scheme orchestrated by a team of some 2,000 Whitehall officials. It was low-grade stuff, with an octane rating of about 72, and motorists were lucky to be able to buy four or five gallons a month, which could allow a carefully driven typical car to cover no more than 120 miles.

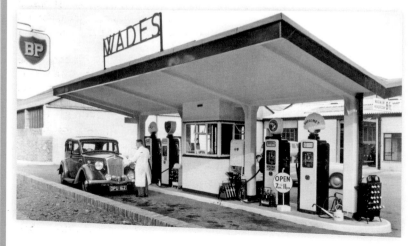

This is Wade's garage in Worthing, Sussex in the very early 1950s, with an attendant permanently stationed on the forecourt between 7 a.m. and 11 p.m.

In 1953, with the nationwide 'pool petrol' scheme axed, familiar brands like Esso returned to garage forecourts. That's a Ford Zodiac Mk I having its windscreen courteously cleaned in Fulham, West London in 1956.

Yet even that meagre allowance appeared generous on 30 June 1942, when a blanket ban on all private motoring was slapped on to the country. From then on, the only cars seen on the roads were driven either by essential workers, like doctors, or else were on official government business.

The basic ration was reintroduced on 1 June 1945, and the new Labour government held firm against all calls to axe it as it struggled to clamp down on the national debt. In fact, it was raised twice in 1946 to allow about 270 miles of monthly driving, but many drivers were livid that all rationing had ended in several European countries, such as France, still devastated by war. And then, on 1 December 1947, the ration was withdrawn altogether and all private motoring once again faced a total lockdown for six months – all in the name of energy conservation and the national balance of payments. So you can well understand the euphoria when the rationing was finally axed – shortly after the Tories almost ousted Labour from power. Queues formed at petrol stations and ration books were joyfully torn up.

Mind you, there was a price to be paid. And that was a massive hike in fuel duty, making petrol prices leap. Duty had remained at 9d (3.75p) on every gallon since 1938. But now it doubled to 1s 6d (7.5p), making the tax take on a 3s gallon fuel exactly 50 per cent.

The petrol companies could finally compete with each other again from 1 February 1953, when the pool petrol system came to an end and familiar brands could restart their

A Vauxhall Cresta PA estate gets the full treatment at a BP forecourt in the very late 1950s. You can see the octane choice between the Regular, Super and Super Plus grades on offer.

battle for customer favour. The big guns were Esso, Shell and BP, with a strong second tier including such now-vanished names as National Benzole, Regent, Cleveland and Power. They all launched marketing campaigns, advertising blitzes and forecourt promotions and regalia, but Esso's tiger character was probably the best recognised corporate motif to emerge.

Most of the petrol firms launched higher-octane 'premium' petrol brands under a variety of sometimes confusing names like 'Extra' and 'Super', and charged an additional 3–4*d* for the privilege of the better engine response they gave. However, in 1954, a fox crept into this complacent henhouse when Yorkshireman Willy Roberts launched his cut-price Jet petrol at a 6*d*

discount for his Premium and 3*d* less for Standard; by 1958 it was being sold through some of the 7 per cent of petrol stations not controlled by the big guns, and a never-ending price war had begun.

Indeed, the total number of petrol-selling outlets across the country continued to grow during the 1950s. Although the total shrank from 35,000 to less than 30,000 between

Thought to be Britain's first self-service petrol outlet, opened in 1960, this amazing circular forecourt in Plymouth, Devon pointed the way to the future of refuelling. In the foreground is an Austin A40 Somerset. (Photo courtesy Photographic Services. Shell International Ltd)

1938 and 1945, it was back up to about 34,000 in '53 and by 1960 there were 37,000 places where you could fill up.

Motorists were directly affected by the so-called Suez crisis in October 1956, when Allied forces invaded Egypt after President Nasser nationalised the Suez Canal there. When the seriousness of the confrontation became obvious, with the disruption to fuel supplies making their laborious sea bound way from the Middle East, petrol rationing was back. From 17 December, coupons were issued permitting, for example, owners of cars up to 1.1 litres a monthly allowance of six gallons, and people driving cars with 2.4-litre engines and above 10.6 gallons. In all cases, this was designed to allow a monthly mileage of 200 and no more. By May 1957, and Britain's embarrassing rout of Egypt, the rationing had ended. In 1958, petrol prices had settled down again to an average of 4s 1d (20.5p) per gallon.

Compared to today, the typical car was something of a chore to maintain. It needed a huge amount of regular mechanical care, and copious lubrication. The very basic Ford Popular of 1953 with its side-

Spacious, customer-friendly forecourts began to be built from the mid 1950s as selling petrol edged towards self-service.

As motoring began to really grow fast in popularity, small backstreet garages had plenty of work, a burgeoning area of small family business.

Main dealer workshops were thriving in this period, and such garages often sold several brands of car. Here a Daimler Conquest and a Humber Super Snipe are vying for mechanical attention.

valve motor, for instance, needed to be serviced every 1,000 miles and have its drivetrain greased in twenty-three places. The Popular 100E that replaced it in 1959 still needed a mechanical inspection every 1,000 miles, although the greasing points had been cut to a 'mere' thirteen! The Austin Princess IV, a brand new model in 1956, also needed attention from the grease gun all over its chassis every 1,000 miles. Even a Jaguar Mk 2 needed servicing every 2,000 miles.

As a consequence, garage workshops were kept extremely busy. True, many people did their own home maintenance, sometimes with the help of useful owner-driver booklets published in huge series by Odhams, Pitman and Cassell – predecessors of the Haynes Manual. Things were made slightly less frustrating for home mechanics in 1948, when hand-cleaning Swarfega arrived, and easier still ten years later when the penetrating oil WD40 (chemist Norm Larsen's fortieth attempt at a 'Water

Displacement' product, hence the name) arrived to free-up stubborn nuts and bolts.

Home car surgery was certainly doable, with a comprehensive toolkit, whether checking oil in the back axle, repairing a puncture, or adjusting a carburettor. But only diehards, really, would tackle the frequent major tasks that many popular cars required to keep going, like re-lining a clutch, adjusting the front suspension, or de-carbonising the engine's innards.

A busy garage workshop at the end of the 1950s, a positive hive of handiwork where mechanical skill was valued.

Looks like new spark plug time for this Morris Minor as the owner looks on, incredulous at the technical wizardry.

The Cassell Book of the

Austin A.30

'SEVEN' (1951-6)
by Ellison Hawks

CASSELL MOTORING SERIES

It was much less of a throwaway era than today. In a time well before electronic gadgets, repairs and overhauls were the labour-intensive norm. Ford, for example, reconditioned worn-out engines at its Dagenham factory, and you could order one to be swapped for the knackered example in your own car, and have it fitted at the dealer. For a Ford Prefect in 1952, an Engine Exchange cost £23 plus fitting, and there were all sorts of other factory-reconditioned parts available too, from fuel pumps to brake shoes; an exchange clutch disc and pressure plate for your Prefect cost £1 10s 6d.

Ellison Hawks wrote dozens of these Cassell home-maintenance books for popular models, helping owners to save money by tackling DIY tasks.

The fact remained that most family cars, even mid-range models, were sparsely equipped, with heaters (often) and radios (usually) as extra-cost options. Hence there was a massive trade in motoring accessories to improve comfort. In its 1957 catalogue, Halfords, with 233 branches all over the country, made a big deal over its range of 1950s man worked hard to keep his car on the road, this chap's overalls showing the devotion he displayed to his humble Ford Prefect.

FACTORY RECONDITIONED ENGINES & PARTS

GENUINE EnFo PARTS & ACCESSORIES

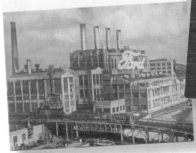

Ford was one of several manufacturers that did a roaring trade in reconditioning original parts for worn-out cars.

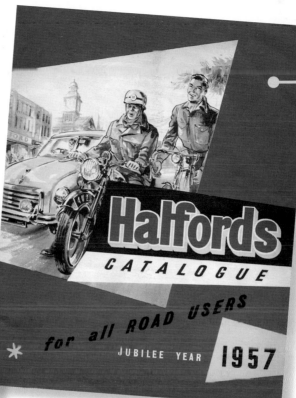

Halfords **CATALOGUE**

for all ROAD USERS

JUBILEE YEAR 1957

Here is the jaunty cover of the 1957 Halfords catalogue, the company covering cars, motorbikes and bicycles much as it still does today.

Bedford Cord seat covers (£5 5s a set for an Austin A30, £6 7s 6d for a Vauxhall Wyvern); they 'save wear on your clothes and preserve the original upholstery'. Meanwhile, the extremely austere nature of many popular British cars is attested to by Halfords' vast range of windscreen washer kits, door handles, wing mirrors, heaters and sun visors on

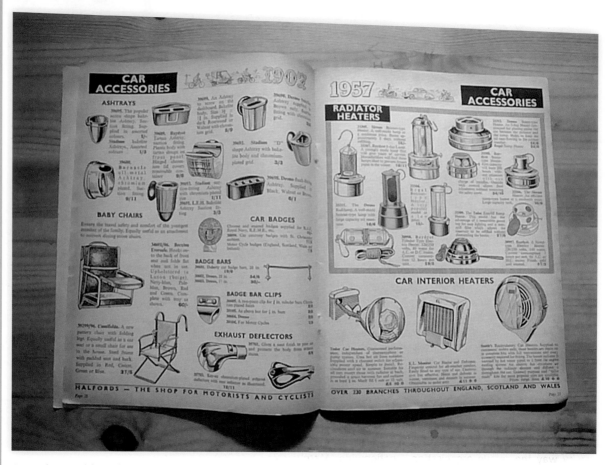

A sample spread from the 1957 Halfords catalogue shows that most of the accessories it sold were far from mere fripperies.

When Hoover introduced the Dustette in 1949 as the world's first handheld vacuum cleaner, cleaning out your car's interior suddenly wasn't such a chore.

A typical cover of *The Motor* magazine in 1955 showed how important parts manufacturers found it to appeal directly to car owners. Any idea who makes the brakes on your current car? Thought not …

offer, as well as all kinds of interior and exterior lights. Picnic trays, ashtrays, coconut mats and chrome wheel discs are some of the few items that hint at fun or style …

In 1950, the newborn Princess Anne became an honorary Automobile Association member – its millionth. This was typical of the catchy way the rescue organisation promoted itself among Britain's massively growing motoring popu-

lation. The previous year, the AA had pioneered the use of two-way radio so its patrols, which previously had to use landlines in AA boxes, could be in constant communication with the control room. It came into its own when the AA night-time breakdown service was launched that year in greater London, and then extended nationwide. Membership, by 1960, reached 2.5 million. AA patrols still used motorcycle combinations, their sidecars crammed with tools, although they were eventually replaced by Mini vans from 1961 onwards. That was also the year when patrols stopped saluting members on the move.

The smaller, more staid and much less progressive RAC didn't join the radio-linked world until 1957, and their patrolmen didn't abandon their quasi-military saluting until 1963.

Signs that sell... *Rootes Products*

Above left: Car showrooms in the 1950s started to be bedecked in neon signs as they battled for customer attention. This brochure was circulated to Hillman and Humber dealers so they could pick the ones that would work on their premises.

Left: In some of the very severe winter weather motorists experienced in Scotland, AA patrols were always willing to lend a hand, here digging out an Austin A40 Somerset from a snowdrift.

Opposite: An RAC patrol brings much-needed stress relief to this stranded female driver of a Wolseley 1500.

Morgan Plus Four, 1950

Phrases like 'a recipe that is almost startling' and 'remarkable acceleration and a high cruising speed' seem like odd verdicts about old Morgans. But that was the critical reaction in 1951 (from *The Autocar* magazine) to an engine transplant that created a Morgan innovation: its first potent performance car.

Where previously small-capacity Coventry-Climax, Ford and Standard engines had provided what Morgan deemed sufficient urge for its sports cars, the Plus Four had a throaty 68bhp of power on tap thanks to the shoehorning-in of the 2.1-litre engine from the otherwise mundane Standard Vanguard. It was the old boys' network in action, as H.F.S. Morgan and Standard's boss Sir John Black had once been apprentices together on the Great Western Railway.

Morgan must have witnessed the export debacle for the Morris Minor, when early cars sent to the USA were found to be too feeble to tackle the hills of San Francisco, irrevocably damaging all sales prospects. If Morgan was going to sell cars in the US – and that was the only way to get allocations of steel to make them with – then they had to be up to the job.

That's why the Plus Four, with its ability to sprint from 0 to 60mph in 18 seconds – believe it, hot stuff seventy years back – and tickle 85mph, not only had a reinforced chassis frame but was subtly longer and wider than its smaller-engined brothers, best to accommodate the already broader beam of the well-fed American sportsman. Also, too, why a decent set of big Girling hydraulic brakes was included. You could have two- or four-seater sports,

The old-fashioned look was no bar to the Plus Four's competition abilities, this one holding off the challenge from a couple of persistent Porsches.

This drophead Coupé body was an unusual option on the Morgan Plus Four chassis, with a roomier, more comfortable cockpit.

or rare two-seater drophead Coupé bodywork.

Morgan won the Team Prize on the 1953 RAC Rally, with Plus Fours continuing their consistently solid showing in everything they contested that year.

Still, after the Triumph TR2-spec 2-litre engine arrived in 1953, with power up by a third and acceleration positively electric at 13.3 seconds for 0–60mph, and the elegant, more wind-cheating cowled frontage was in place, extra potential was unleashed. The most spectacular exponent of that was Chris Lawrence, who crowned an exalted racing career at the wheel of Plus Fours with the pinnacle of Morgan's four-cylinder achievements: a win in the 2-litre GT class at Le Mans in 1962 with a car famously registered TOK 258.

The sloping radiator cowl replaced the former 'flat rad' front on the Plus Four in 1954, certainly making this powerful car a tiny bit more wind-cheating.

WHO LOVED IT?

Already looking decidedly vintage, this big-engined Morgan was still quite a serious sports car for its time, with many gung-ho owners choosing to campaign theirs in races, rallies and trials. It was good value, too. Once again, with pressure to export and bring in foreign currency coming from Whitehall, there weren't many available to British enthusiasts. And in 1953 the Plus Four gained the definitive Morgan 'look' that's still with us today.

This Plus Four, essentially a 1950s version of a pre-war car, pulled off a spectacular finish at Le Mans in 1962, winning the 2-litre GT class.

Austin A30–A35, 1951

All sorts of plans and ideas were hatched to make the 'new Austin Seven' a truly radical shake-up of the economy car. These included cutting-edge thinking such as front-wheel drive, a transversely-mounted engine, rubber suspension and tiny road wheels – pretty much the whole package of the Mini in 1959 but ten years ahead of time. Not only that but American stylists were hired and brought to Longbridge, Birmingham to work on giving the small car an upmarket image and some decidedly un-British design finesse. In the event, Austin management got cold feet, took heed of its cautious dealers and accountants, and all these advanced ideas were abandoned, along with plans for a two-cylinder engine. Still, one fundamental tenet was retained and that was to make the A30 the first Austin with unitary construction, getting rid of a separate chassis for

The Trade Descriptions Act was a long way off, which is probably why the artist working on this brochure painted the occupants so small to make the A30 appear capacious.

What they said at the time

'It is quite lively, and the engine is pleasantly flexible, although it must be admitted that at the top end of the speed range there is a definite impression that parts of the little engine are moving very quickly' – *The Autocar* magazine in 1952 on the £553 A30.

the first time. They did a very good job of it, too. The A30 would be a very durable car, and it tipped the scales at nearly half the weight of an Austin A40 Somerset.

Its engine was an all-new four-cylinder, overhead-cam unit of just 803cc, the first of the extremely long-lived A Series, there was a four-speed gearbox, and the hybrid brakes were hydraulic up-front, mechanical at the back. The styling was changed so that it looked like a baby version of the Somerset, and the car was shortened to save costs. Essentially, what Austin wanted was a large car in miniature – just as the original Seven had been in the 1920s – and that's just how it turned out, complete with conventional suspension and rear-wheel drive.

You could have two or four doors, and it was just about possible to squeeze four adults into the tall and narrow A30 by having no internal door handles to get in the way! To keep costs down, the basic car came with just one windscreen wiper, sun visor and rear brake light; nor was there a heater. But it could do 42mpg and just about touch 70mph. As Austin's answer to the Morris Minor, it was a runaway success.

WHO LOVED IT?

The A30 proved itself just as popular as its arch rival the Morris Minor, the pair giving consumers a great choice of all-British economy cars, and sturdy, dependable introductions to car ownership. Both drove well but in 1952, when Austin and Morris merged to form the British Motor Corporation, they were competitors from the same company. The A30 became the A35 in 1956, with bigger engine and other tweaks, and the van version lived on long after the arrival of the Mini in 1959.

Despite some radical thoughts at its inception, the little Austin turned out to be a conventional car but in miniature; this is an A35 two-door.

Vauxhall Wyvern, Velox & Cresta E Series, 1951

When Ford makes a move in the British car market, its similarly American-owned (by General Motors) competitor Vauxhall usually responds. These days, the two brands are well matched and neck and neck for products on almost every front, but back in the early 1950s it tended to be Ford that led and Vauxhall that trailed.

And so it was with the new Wyvern and Velox models. They were pitched at exactly the same buyers as the Consul and Zephyr respectively, with the lurid Vauxhall Cresta popping up in 1954 to counter the flashy Zephyr Zodiac head-on.

These E Series models, longer and wider than the namesakes they replaced, took their styling inspiration from the 1949 Chevrolet range, and were a little more fussy-looking then the Fords although, like them, they featured unitary construction, overhead-valve engines, independent front suspension and a column gear change.

The Wyvern initially carried over its forebear's 1.5-litre four-cylinder engine, which was shortly changed to a new and much more flexible unit in 1952, upping top speed from 62 to 72mph. The Velox followed the same path but with a 2.2-litre straight six, which was considerably smaller in capacity than the 2.6 in the Ford Zephyr.

Vauxhall tried to keep on-trend with these cars, updating the bonnet

Above: Unusually, the bonnet of the Wyvern and Velox could be opened from the left or right side, or easily detached altogether.

Left: The car is the new Vauxhall Wyvern, which is reflecting in the glory of a BEA Viking at Northolt Airport.

and radiator grille in 1955, when the Velox also gained sleek spats over its rear wheels, slimming the pillars and adding a wraparound rear window, plus replacing 'trafficator' indicator arms with flashing light bulbs, in 1956, and then updating the grille again in '57, when electric windscreen wiper motors were included for the first time. The Cresta evolved in the same way, but it was always distinctive with its two- and some-

times three-tone paint schemes, whitewall tyres, leather seats and bonnet mascot. As a flash motor, nothing else had quite the same aura as a Cresta!

WHO LOVED IT?

Much more so than their Ford equivalents, these Vauxhalls exuded the style of 1950s Detroit, and a lot of buyers liked that confident image very much (with maybe as many potential buyers turned off by it). They were trustworthy cars, if offering a fairly unexciting driving experience. The E Series proved popular in Australia, where it was manufactured for local consumption by General Motors Holden.

This beauty, with its two-tone paint and whitewalls, is the Cresta, Vauxhall's luxury six-cylinder answer to the Ford Zodiac.

RTN 980

Austin A40 Somerset, 1951

Having a separate chassis might not have produced the best car to drive – the lack of torsional strength in the structure, and the weight of the chassis frame itself, blunting the dynamics – but it did mean that updating the bodywork design was a relatively easy and cheap exercise. So four years after the Austin A40 Devon was launched (it had a lot of quality issues, just one of the reasons its export prospects to the USA flickered and died), the team at Austin could use the same frame with an entirely new body.

On top of a much strengthened A40 chassis Austin now plonked a four-door saloon body that was longer and wider, with bigger back doors and what Austin hoped was an overall impression of bulbous modernity. It was, in fact, a slightly shorter and narrower version of the A70 Hereford's body that had been around since 1950. The 1.2-litre overhead-valve engine was the same as the old A40's, but the back axle ratio was higher, so the Somerset (Austin loved using names of English counties for its cars) was a bit more suited to long distances. Still, there was only 42bhp on tap in quite a heavy vehicle, so acceleration was lethargic and the top speed was a paltry 69mph.

Inside there was a bench front seat and column gear change. From late 1952 a 'Somerset Coupé' four-seater convertible was also offered, an easy task for Coventry coachbuilder Carbodies to achieve with the separate chassis as a basis. The two front seats in this were separate so that one or the other could be tipped forward for access to the rear seats, but only 7,243 were sold from a total of 170,306 Somersets built until 1954.

Like the Hillman Minx, this car would make its mark on Japan. A delegation from Nissan came over to see the car being manufactured, and subsequently took out a licence to make the Somerset in their slowly growing Tokyo factory.

It states 'Austin of England' on its side, and wears Austin badges, but this A40 Somerset was built in Japan under licence, by Nissan.

The bulbous shape was a Somerset trademark, but the car still rode on a substantial separate chassis.

What they said at the time

'The A40 is a useful and attractive general-purpose car. It provides comfortable travel for four people, has a useful turn of speed for everyday requirements, and under favourable conditions can average 40mph. The engine is very smooth and silent and there is very little pinking on Pool petrol' – *The Autocar* magazine in 1952 on the £727 A40 Somerset.

WHO LOVED IT?

Austin had a solid and loyal customer base that it had built up in the 1920s and '30s. People trusted its cars and happily accepted whatever it produced. And, in general, they offered decent reliability and good value. However, the Somerset's construction was showing its age, and it was slow. Even Austin recognised that, as it offered an engine head conversion kit to boost the compression ratio and add a little zing to its mediocre performance.

Austin-Healey 100, 1953

The birth of Austin-Healey occurred actually *during* the 1952 London Motor Show at Earls Court. Donald Healey had won the 1931 Monte Carlo Rally in an Invicta, and helped design cars for Riley and Triumph before deciding to open his own company, making Riley-engined Healey sports cars. He tried various designs, which enthusiasts liked a lot, but what he really wanted was a desirable sports car that he could sell to the USA.

His Healey 100, unveiled at Earl's Court, seemed to have the winning combination of drop-dead gorgeous good looks as a ground-hugging two-seater roadster, and affordable power aplenty from the 2.6-litre four-cylinder Austin engine.

Recognising the car's enormous potential and seizing the moment, Austin boss Sir Leonard Lord took Healey out for dinner on the eve of the show and persuaded him to let Austin build and sell the cars. Healey agreed, and the Austin-Healey marque was created. It was essentially a licensing deal, with Healey receiving a royalty on every car Austin sold in exchange for the reflected glory of using his name.

Healey had considered making twenty of the cars a week, but Austin planned for ten times that number, with Jensen manufacturing the bodies and the cars assembled at Longbridge.

The 100 in the car's title referred to its top speed of 100+mph. Indeed, it was the world's cheapest 100mph sports car, and with 90bhp on tap in a lightweight two-seater, acceleration was thrilling. The rakish 100, on wire wheels and with a fold-flat windscreen, could hit 60mph in under 10 seconds. The normal bottom gear was blanked off, but there was overdrive on the top two of the remaining three (a four-speed transmission with overdrive arrived in 1955). Unusually, a heater was standard equipment!

In 1953, an ordinary Austin-Healey 100/4 averaged 103.94mph in a 5,000km endurance demonstration

Donald Healey finally hit the jackpot with his Austin-Healey 100 sports car – the first affordable 100mph model.

at the Bonneville Salt Flats in Utah, USA. Healey himself offered many accessories including a tuning kit, and also made a lightweight 100S competition version, and a 110bhp road version of it, the 100M. Total production of the 100/4 was 14,634. The 100-Six of 1956 gained BMC's new six-cylinder 2,639cc engine, plus two tiny children's seats in the back, while the 1959 3000 was boosted to 2,912cc.

WHO LOVED IT?

This was the car every sports car fan wanted to get his hands on because it was cheaper than a Jaguar yet so much more punchy and stylish than an MG, but only some 1,400 cars actually reached British buyers, because 90 per cent of the 14,600 built went for export, overwhelmingly to those lucky blighters in the USA.

What they said at the time

'Corners which previously were a test of skill are taken as fast as traffic conditions will allow, so easily as to become almost insignificant. For a "real" sensation of cornering it is necessary to find open road bends on which to drive faster than the usual family car's cruising speed' – *The Motor* magazine in September 1953 on the £1,063 Austin-Healey 100.

Left-hand drive was typical on the Austin-Healey 100 because the vast majority were destined for export to the USA.

Daimler Conquest, 1953

The story of Daimler in the 1950s is a complex tale of steady decline, as its largely hand-built, old-fashioned cars struggled at the same time as Jaguar's superb-to-drive production-line models thrived.

The 1953 Conquest was the old-established Coventry firm's best shot at offering something relevant to the era, when chauffeurs were dwindling and owner-drivers were starting to demand driving enjoyment.

It was priced, rather jocularly, at £1,066 before purchase tax was added. However, this Daimler bore little relation to the company's big limos and formal saloons because it was actually a clever development of a car made by Lanchester, a Daimler subsidiary.

So the Conquest used the chassis and steel-framed body of the Lanchester Leda, complete with independent front suspension by torsion bars (good old leaf springs at the back), and a six-cylinder, 2.5-litre enlargement of the Leda's four-cylinder engine, with 75bhp on tap. Both cars shared a single-shot chassis lubrication system and hydraulic front/mechanical rear brakes. Telescopic dampers all round afforded a comfortable ride.

The bodies were near-identical, but on the Daimler the finish and ambience was more upmarket.

Even Daimler realised this high-quality car offered slow and uninspiring performance, which is why in 1954 they offered a souped-up edition called the Conquest Century in honour of the 100bhp now coaxed from an engine endowed with an aluminium cylinder head, higher compression, larger valves and twin carburettors. 'Century' might also have signified 100mph, which the upright car may conceivably have been capable of downhill with a following wind; 90mph was the reality.

These cars were fastidiously built but were starting to feel like living antiques, especially as the standard transmission was Daimler's venerable four-speed pre-selector gearbox with a fluid flywheel, a system designed for olden days when drivers wanted to make as few gear changes as possible. A modern Borg Warner automatic and more space in the cramped rear seats by 1956 were concessions to modernity that hardly changed the car's character. Similarly, the various Convertible and Roadster editions seemed like feeble responses to the

The Conquest Century photographed at the time of the introduction of automatic transmission as a new option.

likes of Jaguar and Mercedes-Benz. Daimler tried cutting its prices but it was drifting towards oblivion and, indeed, Jaguar bought the company out in 1960, two years after the last Conquest, a Century, had been built. Precisely 4,568 Daimler Conquest saloons were sold, plus 4,818 Conquest Centurys and around 450 other Roadsters and Dropheads.

What they said at the time

'The gears are selected by a lever mounted on the steering column, but the actual engagement is performed by the pedal which is placed in the position usually occupied by the clutch pedal. Any desired gear can be selected by hand or pre-selected – in anticipation of requirements – but the change will not take place until the pedal is operated' – *The Autocar* magazine in 1953 on the £,1511 Conquest.

WHO LOVED IT?

A very particular type of old-fashioned, upper-middle-class, well-off Brit, no doubt working in the professions, and perhaps with a family affinity to Daimlers that stretched back decades and admired the marque's long-standing ties to the Royal Family, and its other links to the days of Empire. Certainly most Daimler owners regarded Jaguars as vulgar and a foreign car as an absolute no-no. But the rest of the world was moving on.

Film star Norman Wisdom takes delivery of his brand new Conquest Roadster at the Daimler factory in Coventry.

Ford Anglia & Prefect 100E Series, 1953

These names were some of the most familiar on Britain's roads, but the cars themselves were almost totally new. Ford really went to town in making this pair thoroughly modern but also affordable and cheap to run.

A lot of the hardware aped the larger Ford Consul in being a full monocoque structure with MacPherson strut independent front suspension, robust half-elliptic leaf springs at the rear, and Girling hydraulic brakes. The three-speed gear change was floor-mounted, and both cars drew their motive power from a reworked 1.2-litre 36bhp engine, still side-valve but given bigger inlet valves, a raised compression ratio, and an engine-driven pump to assist with cooling.

The exterior styling was revolutionary for anyone used to the somewhat perpendicular outgoing Anglia and Prefect. It was a neat and pleasant shape with a 'three-box' profile, offering two doors for the Anglia and four small ones for the Prefect on the same wheelbase. At first the Anglia's grille featured horizontal bars and the Prefect vertical ones, but a 1957 refresh endowed them both with lattice-patterned grilles.

Inside, the cars had separate front seats, tipping in the Anglia to allow access to the rear, and although upholstery was sticky PVC plastic and equipment sparse – no heater or radio – there was an opening glovebox and there was even the option of a rather primitive two-speed automatic transmission. Two windscreen wipers now came as standard, although the vacuum-powered mechanism that made them work was prone to slowing right down on steep hills or under sudden acceleration. The electrical system itself was a 12-volt one.

They were quite good to drive, although hardly quick, with a widened track over their forebears improving roadholding, and the steering feeling precise and balanced. And anyone wanting a bit more cargo space could go for two estate car models. The Escort was the companion model to the Anglia and the slightly more upmarket Squire equated to the Prefect, although both were actually derived from the little 100E Thames van.

Morris dancers take a break to admire the new Ford Anglia 100E.

The Anglia (front) and Prefect, here seen being admired on an elegant London street, were probably Britain's most popular cars of the 1950s.

WHO LOVED IT?

Although no car bestsellers' chart was released in the UK until 1965, it's likely these small Fords were often Britain's best-selling models in the mid 1950s. With almost half-a-million examples shifted, it was easy to see why; the 30mpg fuel economy went down well with punters, although acceleration was leisurely at about 30 seconds for the 0–60mph dash, with a top speed of 70mph.

What they said at the time

'The behaviour of the car on corners is outstandingly good. Due to fairly high gearing and the small amount of sponginess in the steering linkage, control is both accurate and almost immediate, but the effort required on the wheel is at a minimum and there is no unpleasant reaction to rough surfaces' – The Motor magazine in May 1954 on the £511 Anglia.

Mercedes-Benz 180, 190 & 220, 1953

These solid-looking cars really established Merc's credentials for making comfortable but tough medium-sized saloons.

The modern styling, with traces of separate mudguards all but banished, gained the series the German nickname of *Ponton*, meaning pontoon, or full-width. In fact, the body structure was unitary, losing a separate chassis, and several hundred cars were built daily at the Sindelfingen plant just outside Stuttgart, where it took 1,500 minutes between the first steel being cut to the completed car rolling off the production line.

The early 180 model had a wheezy 1.8-litre side-valve engine, updated to a much more flexible overhead-camshaft unit in 1957. There was also the 190, introduced in 1956, which offered the same 75bhp 1.9-litre motor and fully-synchromesh gearbox as the Mercedes 190SL roadster, and quite a bit more chrome trim in its upmarket finish. Sliding Webasto sunroofs were available in both fabric and metal.

The 190 was the most frequently seen of these cars in the UK, but if you wanted even more power and prestige then there was also the 220 series using the same bodyshell, of which the 220S with its twin-carb engine was a 100mph car.

However, it's the diesel models that merit special mention. Mercedes had pioneered diesel power in passenger cars in the 1930s and the diesel 180 and 190 (the latter not sold in Britain) really helped to popularise it. In 1978, Mercedes in the US located a 1957 180D that had covered almost 1.2 million miles, and had it listed in the *Guinness Book of Records* as the 'world's most durable car'.

Commonly known as the *Ponton* for their pontoon-like full-width styling, the new Mercs were comfortable and modern.

As long-distance touring cars these Mercedes-Benz models were unbeatable, mostly because they were so well engineered.

WHO LOVED IT?

They found favour all over the world, often as taxis but just as often as appropriately sober transport for officials and businessmen, because they were engineered to what might have been termed 'world standards' of integrity, and found buyers in 136 different countries.

What they said at the time

'For the mature yet keen long-distance motorist, interested more in refinement than sparkling acceleration, and seeking a car which should give good service over a considerable number of years, this model even at its duty-paid British price has real attractions' – *The Motor* magazine in June 1954 on the £1,694 180.

MG Magnette ZA & ZB, 1953

In 1952, sister British Motor Corporation marque Wolseley had launched its new small saloon, the well-finished but somewhat underwhelming Four-Forty-Four, and it was immediately obvious that the Magnette was closely based on that car. MG, though, had recruited Gerald Palmer, designer of the Jowett Javelin, to create the sporting MG edition, and he oversaw a remarkable transformation.

Out went the Wolseley's 1.25-litre engine from the old MG TD and in its place was BMC's all-new 1.6-litre B Series motor; with its twin SU carburettors, the unit delivered a peppy 60bhp, with a floor-mounted gear change instead of the Wolseley's cumbersome column-mounted lever. Big 10-inch drum brakes did the stopping job adequately, and the first cars came with Pirelli's new, state-of-the-art Cinturato tyres.

One of the Wolseley's better features, its rack-and-pinion steering, was retained, but Palmer lowered the Magnette's suspension to make the car that bit more road-hugging. The Magnette had a lovely interior with a wooden dashboard and door cappings, and leather-faced seats.

Palmer also managed a visual makeover to make the car look sleeker, with 'go-faster' chrome flashes hugging the front wheel arches, and slightly different profiles for the front and rear wings. A lower bonnet line was matched by a boot profile that dispensed with the Wolseley's upright number plate in the centre.

This was a pleasant and sporty little saloon that drove and behaved very satisfyingly. MG also made sure it kept the car on the pace, adding extra engine power in 1956 (top speed jumped from 80 to 86mph) and interior refinements, and there was also a trendy Varitone model with a bigger rear window and a two-tone paint job. These cars were on sale until 1958.

The second-generation Magnette was called the Varitone for its dual colour scheme, and also featured a wraparound rear window for better visibility.

WHO LOVED IT?

Despite some grumbles from MG purists about the quantity of Austin-related BMC parts in this example of their beloved marque, there were plenty of takers for this brand of quality British sports saloon, one of the best affordable options this side of a Jaguar. Almost 40,000 Magnettes found buyers. Its eagerness and solidity would ultimately see many end their days on the banger racing track, rendering them quite rare today.

What they said at the time

'The engine's cheerful ability to rev is well balanced by the roadholding of the car, which is remarkable indeed. Wet roads or dry make little difference to its performance. The driving position is just right. A tall man does not feel cramped after a long, fast journey' – *The Autocar* in November 1954 on the £914 Magnette ZA.

If you couldn't run to a Jaguar then the Magnette, seen here in original ZA form, was the next best thing as an enjoyable sports saloon.

Reliant Regal, 1953

The Reliant Motor Company first revealed its intention to become a carmaker in 1951, and two years later the first deliveries began of its Regal, a four-seater convertible.

It was, naturally, a three-wheeler. In fact, the first Regals were derived directly from the Regent van that Reliant had been building, in constantly updated form, since 1935. Although these weird-looking motorised tricycles for local deliveries started out with V-twin motorbike engines, Reliant had started using the more refined four-cylinder 747cc water-cooled engine from the Austin Seven in 1938, and when Austin announced that this ancient side-valve motor would be discontinued, Reliant designed a close copy, which it manufactured itself, to become self-sufficient for power units.

The big plus of these vans had been that they were taxed as motorbikes, which, along with their very light weight, meant they could be run on a shoestring by small businesses and large fleets alike. This penny-pinching mindset was conferred to the passenger car edition, which featured a simple aluminium-panelled body on a wooden frame but with the Regent chassis largely unchanged.

To optimise performance, Reliant was constantly seeking ways to make the Regal lighter, which was why is started to fit some glass-fibre panels as early as 1954. Two years later and the Mk III Regal's entire body was of the plastic wonder material, which now included a roof to turn it into a proper family saloon, and for the following three series, made up to 1962, the company worked hard to make its little car a decent alternative to a four-wheeler. The side-valve engine might have seemed a millstone in a conventional car, but in the featherweight Regal it allowed a reasonably lively response, even if the non-synchromesh gearbox was a little off-putting, the ride rough, and the handling skittish.

No equivalent Car can offer so much
★ Up to the minute styling.
★ Comfortable four seater.
★ Economy — 50 m.p.g.
★ Performance — 65 m.p.h.

★ 4 cylinder water-cooled engine
★ Hydraulic brakes on all wheels.
★ Tubeless tyres.

A page from the brochure for the Regal Mk III listing the Reliant's many ownership benefits; this is the hardtop model, now all glass-fibre bodied.

What they said at the time

'In performance it is some 27 per cent faster than the average of current three-wheelers we have tested, and accelerates from rest to 40mph through the gears in less than half the time. Compared with the cheapest normal four-wheeler its performance is almost identical in both these respects' – *The Motor* magazine in June 1957 on the £430 Regal hardtop.

Top left: The original Regal was a tiny little four-seater convertible of the most basic nature, but buyers loved its thrift.

Top right: An illustration of a Mk III chassis from the brochure, showing the simple but effective underpinnings of the three-wheeler.

Below right: The Mk III Regal could still be had as a convertible for those who enjoyed economy motoring under a blazing sky.

WHO LOVED IT?

With minimal running costs but vaguely car-like levels of refinement, the Regal had some appeal to car drivers on a tight budget. But its main market was among young families where, in the days before the kids arrived, mum and dad had a motorbike or motorcycle-and-sidecar combination. No extra driving test needed to be taken, and all the running costs were on a par with a large bike. Regals were especially popular in Britain's Midlands and the North, where the coal-mining and steelmaking industries were based.

1950s
Dream Cars

While all around was doom and gloom in the motoring world, the late 1940s – the slip road into the 1950s car world – saw some real excitement for British enthusiasts with a pair of inspiring home-grown products.

First off the starting grid was the Healey 2.4-litre, an exciting new model from sports-car racer and engineer Donald Healey. Although the powerful four-cylinder, 2.4-litre engine came from Riley, the rest of the car was all new. Healey himself demonstrated the sleek saloon model on a super-straight piece of Belgian road called the Jabbeke Highway in 1947 to prove this was a 110mph car, thanks to its clever engineering and wind-cheating shape. This made it the fastest production car in the world.

Yet the Healey was only just getting into limited production when, at the London Motor Show in 1948, Jaguar stole its thunder with the utterly sensational XK120

The man himself, Donald Healey, at the wheel of a prototype example of his Healey 2.4-litre.

The XK120 was the most exciting sports car in the world, featuring Jaguar's brand new XK six-cylinder twin-cam engine.

Jaguar's team at Jabbeke in Belgium, where this largely standard XK120 managed to reach 132mph – astonishingly fast for the time.

two-seater. Not only was it breathtakingly gorgeous, but its tremendous all-new 3.4-litre XK twin-cam engine could propel the roadster to 120mph. Once again the company went to Jabbeke in 1949 to prove the car's worth, and there test driver Ron 'Soapy' Sutton more than did the business, reaching 132mph.

Healey, despite its cars' excellent reputation, limped along as a marque, and Donald Healey would only hit big-time success when he teamed up with Austin for the Austin-Healey 100 (see page 80). Jaguar, on the other hand, used the XK120 to captivate American customers and make the US its number one export territory. Progressively and carefully developed, it became the XK140 in 1954 and then the XK150 in 1958, remaining among the most powerful British sports cars available; the XK120C, or C-type, won at Le Mans twice, followed by a hat-trick of victories there for the subsequent D-type.

Bristol was another noteworthy manufacturer, a new enterprise from the eponymous aircraft manufacturer. The first Bristol car was the 400, and the design was based entirely on the BMW 327, which had been taken from the Germans as 'reparation' after the war. After a couple of years, Bristol designed its own bodywork with help from its own aerodynamics boffins and Italian coach-builder Touring. These 401 and 403 models established Bristols as some of the finest cars you could buy, albeit at a substantial price, and the 404, 405 and 406 derivatives launched throughout the decade were all highly desirable.

Bristol's development of BMW's straight-six 2-litre engine found a further home under the bonnet of the delightful AC Ace, another British sports car that arrived in 1953 and would prove to be a formidable challenger on the race tracks, as well as forming the basis for the fearsome AC Cobra of the '50s.

Jaguar's XK sports cars evolved during the 1950s to keep them desirable; this is the XK150 Roadster.

The Bristol 403
mixed science,
in the form of
aerodynamics
and lightweight
construction,
with a wonderful
2-litre six-
cylinder engine.

A mainstay of sports car racing during the 1950s,
the pretty AC Ace was also a delight to drive on
the road.

The Aston Martin chronology throughout the decade began with the DB2 in 1950, a car that had already been proven as a beefy goer in sports-racing car events even before it went on sale. At its heart was a 2.6-litre straight-six engine designed by the legendary W.O. Bentley, while the aura was of high performance in a sumptuously finished environment of wood and leather. The series saw all manner of improvements, including the fitment of a hatchback tailgate and front disc brakes, until the DB4 arrived in 1958.

Bentley itself provided one of the most desirable GT cars in the world with the Continental version of its R-Type. Lightweight chassis, lowered steering and a tuned engine shrugged off the usual Rolls-Royce/Bentley haughtiness,

Perhaps the ultimate in British luxury sports cars of the early 1950s, the Aston Martin DB2 was race-bred and wonderfully appointed.

and the absolutely beautiful handmade bodywork was very stable at high speeds while also providing one of the most luxurious of passenger compartments then available.

Other powerful and characterful British sporting cars included the Alvis TC108G/TD21 series from 1955 and the glass-fibre-clothed Jensen 541 from '53. There was nothing very dream car like from old-established Daimler, although its 1948 DB18 Special Sports had a certain charm and the 1953 Conquest Roadster was the first vaguely sporting car the company had devised since 1908.

However, what Daimler did offer every year throughout the early 1950s was a show car that wowed the crowds at the annual motor show. With names like Silver Flash, Golden Zebra, Green Goddess and Blue Clover, they were

There was a special chassis for the Bentley R-type Continental, with lower radiator grille and steering, and stunning aluminium bodywork.

Daimler built a series of show cars, including this one called Golden Zebra in 1955, that really caught the public's imagination. And, yes, the 'chrome' is indeed all gold-plated.

This Rolls-Royce Silver Wraith, the ultimate in 1950s limos, was once the property of chirpy film star George Formby.

flamboyant of line and glitteringly over the top in detail and finish. And the public loved them.

For many, the idea of a 1950s dream car was an elegant limousine in which they could be chauffeured, and Daimler was right up there with its straight-eight-engined (Britain's last engine of this type) DE36 models from 1946–53, which were owned by no less than seven royal families, and then the subsequent six-cylinder Regina/DK400 series.

However, the ultimate car had, really, long been a Rolls-Royce, and the Silver Wraith was the most baronial vehicle on sale, especially when given a vast and imposing body by one of several coachbuilders. For many, though, the Bentley R-Type/Rolls Silver Dawn was a perfectly adequate way of expressing their wealth, and when the opulent and handsome Rolls Silver Cloud/Bentley S Series made its debut in 1955 the duo truly cemented desire for what they called the 'best car in the world'. But if that was just too formal for you then there

Rolls-Royce pitched its Silver Cloud of 1955 at the increasing number of customers who now preferred to drive rather than be chauffeured.

A marvellous car, and the first anywhere with a V6 engine, this Lancia Aurelia was imported to the UK in small numbers starting in 1953.

America went mad for the Ford Thunderbird in 1954 but very few came to Britain. Still, at least the Consul Mk II looked a *bit* like it …

was always the good-looking and slightly sportier Lagonda 3-litre; the Duke of Edinburgh was a big fan of that.

You will notice that all these mouth-watering machines mentioned so far are British. A total sales ban on foreign cars followed by a period of punishing import tariffs meant supplies of sports and luxury cars made beyond these shores were non-existent until the mid 1950s. One of the first non-domestic 'exotic' models to find favour here was the delectable Lancia Aurelia B20 GT, sold in Britain in very small numbers from 1953; perhaps it was no coincidence because this car, with its complex V6 engine, was produced only with right-hand drive anyway! Soon it would be joined in the line-up for high-net-worth individuals by exclusively select numbers of France's Facel Vega FV and HK500, with American Chrysler V8 power, the new Ferrari 250 GT from Italy and, at the very tail end of the 1950s, the first few examples of the 3500GT, Maserati's exciting new road car.

The Cadillacs and Lincolns, the Ford Thunderbirds and Chevrolet Corvettes, and the Chryslers and Oldsmobiles

Chevrolet's Corvette made its debut in 1953, bringing with it the novelty of glass-fibre bodywork; there were never any official UK imports, though.

that lit up American roads variously with their chrome, fins and sometimes 20ft length were cars we were familiar with chiefly through reading magazines and watching American movies. A very small number found their way to the UK, and actually seeing a modern American car anywhere away from the US Embassy in London's Grosvenor Square was quite an event.

Britain's former foes, the Germans, were also back in the UK by 1954, with imports of new Mercedes-Benz cars starting once again, a trickle of BMWs, and also the first small consignments of a funny little rear-engined Coupé called a Porsche.

While the BMW 501 saloon, the 503 Coupé and the 507 roadster were impressive, and the Porsche 356 was getting rave reviews, it was the Mercedes-Benz 300SL, with its fuel-injected engine and awe-inspiring lift-up gull-wing doors, that caused most excitement. It was, in effect, the first true 'supercar', and had shown its storming performance in ball-breaking events like the Le Mans 24-Hours and Carrera Panamericana endurance races.

On the other hand, many people were impressed by the svelte and stylish lines of the Volkswagen Karmann Ghia, and that had hardly any power at all, much less any racing pedigree.

You couldn't fail to be awed by the gull-wing doors on the Mercedes-Benz 300SL, as much as by its fuel-injected high performance.

The Porsche 356 was new from Germany, a fascinating car derived from the VW Beetle but now forging its own identity.

This Roadster version of the 300SL was rather more practical than the gull-wing, and super-wealthy British buyers ordered a few of them.

Not as feisty as a Porsche but a whole lot more sleek than a 'Beetle' saloon; this is the Volkswagen Karmann-Ghia in Coupé and cabriolet forms.

Standard Eight & Ten, 1953

After a few false dawns with the sometimes unreliable Vanguard and the slightly weird, slow-selling Mayflower, the Standard-Triumph organisation decided it needed something simple and cheap to lure British people into its dealers' showrooms. And these Standards certainly were short on frills and big on thrift.

With Austin, Ford and Morris raising the bar with monocoque construction, independent front suspension and (mostly) reasonably responsive overhead-valve engines, there was no way these small family saloons could do without those attributes. And everything on the Eight was newly designed. This included the 26bhp (upped to 30bhp in 1957) 803cc engine and the four-speed gearbox with synchromesh on the upper three speeds.

However, the idea was to position the car at well below the price of a Morris Minor, and the most basic Eight at £491 on the road was £51 less. For this, you basically got four wheels, four seats, a roof and an engine. The Eight was stripped to the bone, with a single windscreen wiper, no inner door trims, no heater, virtually no chrome trim, sliding windows, and there wasn't even an external boot lid – you had to shove your luggage into the cargo hold by folding down the back seat.

This scrimping really went too far for most. Even Standard-Triumph's

What they said at the time

'The increase in cylinder bore diameter of 5mm provides the Ten with an extra 7bhp, and although it turns the scale at 1cwt more than the Eight, the net result is a much more lively car in acceleration and maximum speed. This liveliness is obtained at the cost of a reduction of up to eight in the total miles which can be covered on a gallon of fuel' – *The Autocar* magazine in December 1954 on the £580 Ten.

Standing by the new Standard Eight is the mercurial Sir John Black, head of the company, with a very blunt manner …

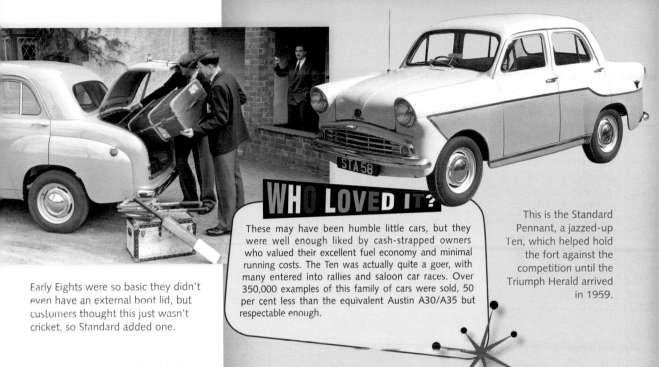

Early Eights were so basic they didn't even have an external boot lid, but customers thought this just wasn't cricket, so Standard added one.

WHO LOVED IT?

These may have been humble little cars, but they were well enough liked by cash-strapped owners who valued their excellent fuel economy and minimal running costs. The Ten was actually quite a goer, with many entered into rallies and saloon car races. Over 350,000 examples of this family of cars were sold, 50 per cent less than the equivalent Austin A30/A35 but respectable enough.

This is the Standard Pennant, a jazzed-up Ten, which helped hold the fort against the competition until the Triumph Herald arrived in 1959.

booming boss Sir John Black once described the cars as the 'Belsen line' because they were so austere. Buyers tended to opt for the slightly more costly De Luxe, and by 1957 even the standard car had wind-down windows and an opening boot.

Maybe surprisingly, and despite being capable of just 61mph, the Eight was quite spritely, with a light clutch and precise steering, and it felt reasonably refined too, lacking vibration or racket. What mattered was that it could achieve 43mpg. The 948cc Standard Ten of 1954 added quite a good measure of extra performance, and the related spin-off models like the Companion estate and the two-tone Pennant with its tail fins and hooded headlights helped form an entire range, which lasted until 1961, two years after the Triumph Herald had largely replaced these compact Standards.

Volkswagen 'Export' Saloon, 1953

It was rejected by Britain's motor industry as unsaleable but, nevertheless, put into mass production with the help of the British Army in its post-war rebuild of West Germany. So the 'Volks Wagen' (People's Car) started rolling off the Wolfsburg lines in 1945, at first reserved for customers like the German Post Office and the Allied occupational forces. The attributes of reliability and engineering rigour were already abundantly evident in this rear-engined, air-cooled four-seater saloon with its distinctively curvaceous appearance.

British soldiers could buy a Volkswagen for a concessionary £100 and take it home, but very few chose to.

The four-cylinder engine of 1,131cc was positioned horizontally at the back, produced 25bhp of power at 3,300rpm, and was air-cooled and so wouldn't ice up in winter or overheat in summer. Some rear-engined cars later developed a scary reputation for stability, but the VW's gutlessness and modest bulk – the whole car weighed just 720kg – made it pretty foolproof.

There were a few teething problems, but quick-witted managers put a strict regime in place focusing upon the quality of components *before* the cars were actually assembled. Volkswagen launched its 'Export' model in 1949 (the Beetle name would not arrive, officially, until the late 1960s), with hydraulic brakes, damped steering, a choice of bright paint colours, chrome bumpers, and a more comfortable interior.

With manufacturing standards and comfort taken care of, Volkswagen's engineers next looked at the car's modest power output and decided to give it a boost. The result was the new 1200 model in 1954, with an enlarged 1,192cc engine producing 30bhp, which meant a top speed increase to 70mph.

The one millionth VW was built on 8 August 1955. There was huge celebration at all Volkswagen outposts, not least of these Volkswagen of America Inc., which opened for business that year and became the biggest US car importer as it instantly overtook the previous leader – Britain's very own Austin.

Golden moment: this specially-painted Volkswagen was the millionth example of the car to be built on 8 August 1955.

A British-market Volkswagen 1200 in about 1960 with the more practical rectangular rear window, a 34bhp engine and – finally – synchromesh on first gear.

What they said at the time

'It's easy for any driver to obtain the best performance from the car. The synchromesh cannot be beaten, either on slow changes or on snap full-throttle changes; the gears always engage silently and easily. A roadworthy, robust small car ... It gives a good performance without effort' – *The Autocar* magazine in 1953 on the £439 Export Saloon.

Major Ivan Hirst at a pivotal moment in the British Army's efforts to get the Volkswagen into proper production after the Second World War.

Triumph TR2 & TR3, *1953*

It's funny, really, to recall that Triumph cars were originally a sideline for the eponymous motorbike maker that is so succesful again today. In just over sixty years, 1923 to 1984, they came and went, and the marque's career was never smooth. Occasionally, however, Triumph produced a much-loved car. Like the TR2.

I choose my words carefully. 'Much loved' the TR2 certainly was. But like most other Triumphs, 'great' would surpass the truth.

Company head Sir John Black wanted a 2-litre sports car to beat MG at its own game, but the prototype was created so cheaply, using so many outdated parts, that Ken Richardson,

who ran the company's motor sport activities, declared it a 'death trap' and 'the most awful car I've ever driven in my life … The chassis, brakes and steering are all wrong.'

So Richardson himself was tasked with sorting the car out, with just eight months to get it up to scratch for release to the public in May 1953.

The main improvement was to design a straightforward ladder-type chassis to replace the bendy old bedstead the TR1 had used. The company's stylists – spurred on by the snappy styling of the rival Austin-Healey 100 – replaced the TR1's runty tail with a more graceful, tapering rear end, adding a boot lid

and a locker for the spare wheel. Then Richardson began the arduous, night-and-day process of fettling the car's suspension, steering, brakes and gearbox until it resembled a proper sports car.

Through Herculean effort, the TR2 hit the shops in July 1953 at £787.

Its frills were few. The hood and upholstery were plastic, and unless you paid extra for a heater it was horribly draughty with the hood and flimsy side-screens up. There were also plenty of irksome faults, like doors that opened too low and scraped on kerbstones and the large steering wheel that skimmed the thighs.

The TR2 was a fast and fun sports car, but an awful lot of work was required to rid the prototype of its deathtrap reputation.

The new owner of a TR2 looks pleased with himself, as his wife and possibly mother-in-law gaze on admiringly too.

Yet its 2-litre, twin-carburettor engine gave a lusty 90bhp, thanks to tuning experts at racing car company BRM. It returned an excellent 35mpg yet licked 108mph with optional overdrive, and could manage 60mph from standstill in under 12 seconds – all down to a low 1,888lb weight.

WHO LOVED IT?

Through spirited and manly performance, this sports car really endeared itself to the sports jacket brigade. A one-two in the 1954 RAC Rally helped bestow widespread credibility. The TR line proved a great success; the TR2 became the TR3 in 1956 after 8,628 had been sold, many in the USA, and its hearty, homespun spirit survived until the last TR6 was built twenty years later.

The TR3 made a gutsy rally car, seen here going great guns on the Liège-Rome-Liège Rally in 1958.

What they said at the time

'Although we have felt obliged to criticise some details and characteristics in quite emphatic terms, we nevertheless rate this as not merely the best sports car available at its price, but also as one of the most promising new models which has been introduced in recent years' – *The Motor* magazine in April 1954 on the £900 TR2.

Austin A50–A105, 1954

It was all change yet again on the style front for Austin's mid-range saloons as the Somerset and Hereford were replaced with models that swapped county imagery for that of centres of institutional power, as the A40/A50 Cambridge and the A90 Westminster took their places.

All the cars enjoyed a similar neat and modern design treatment, with the suggestion of separate wings replaced by light, pressed-in styling lines. They were, perhaps, a little dull stylistically, but underneath they all employed unitary construction, and so were a quantum leap ahead of the previous separate chassis/body generation. They would, though, be the very last Austin-brand cars from BMC with their own unique body shape.

The A40 Cambridge (offered only until 1956) had a 1.2-litre four-cylinder motor, the A50 Cambridge a 1.5-litre – the new BMC B-Series unit – and the very slightly wider and longer A90 Westminster had the New C-Series 2.6-litre straight-six, with a lusty 85bhp on tap. The A90 was the first really rapid Austin, easily capable of 75mph cruising without getting hot and bothered; it had a four-speed gearbox with, later on, optional overdrive, and put up a remarkably good showing in on-track saloon car racing, where it could snap at the heels of a Jaguar Mk VII, and in rallying, while adventurer Richard Pape drove one 17,500 miles from the North Cape of Norway to Cape Town, South Africa, surviving a head-on collision. Aware that the car had image potential, Austin added a 102bhp A105 Westminster in May 1956, with twin carbs and two-tone paintwork.

For the 1957 season, all these cars gained a bigger boot, which also provided more graceful looks, and an estate car edition of the A95 was added to the range.

Silverstone 1958 and ace driver Jack Sears in his A90 Westminster does a masterful job of holding off Jeff Uren in a Ford Zephyr Mk II in a production saloon car race; notice, no roll cages or helmets then.

'Speeds of the order of which this car is capable are undesirable unless they can be used in safety, and on this score the Austin designers have achieved a happy compromise between comfort and the stability needed for high performance. The suspension is firm, but not to the extent of giving a bumpy ride. The steering, light and accurate' – *The Autocar* magazine in June 1955 on the £834 Austin A90 Westminster.

WHO LOVED IT?

This range of models was a major step up from their predecessors in most important areas. They were both decent to drive and also built like tanks, and so provided plenty of satisfaction as family cars to the middle classes, even if the equivalent Ford Consuls and Zephyrs probably had the edge on them for both modern style and driving pleasure.

The A50 Cambridge was another Austin to go into production in Japan as Nissan cut its teeth as a carmaker with the licence-built British family car.

Morris Cowley, Oxford & Isis, 1954

The long-anticipated merger in 1952 of the Austin Motor Company and the Nuffield Organisation (purveyor of Morris, MG, Riley and Wolseley cars) – the first really important consolidation of a British motor industry under siege from foreign competition – gave us the giant British Motor Corporation. Its rosette logo started to pop up here and there among the group's many activities, and there was an immediate rationalisation of engines. But the new company's cars were still sold by two massive chains of dealers, and both wanted brand-specific new models to sell.

So just as Austin agents were given the Cambridge and Westminster cars detailed on the previous pages, now it was the Morris network's turn for some fresh fare. The direct equivalents were a 1.2-litre Cowley, a 1.5-litre Oxford, and a 2.6-litre Isis employing the same power units as the Austin trio but in a completely different body/chassis unit, with its torsion-bar front independent suspension and hydraulic drum brakes. And it wasn't an especially attractive body at that, being decidedly dumpy. At least a heater was standard equipment on the Oxford, unusual for the period.

These cars suffered a slightly uncomfortable driving position thanks to an offset steering column. Only

THE MORRIS COWLEY
BRITAIN'S FIRST FAMILY CAR IN PERFORMANCE, ROOMINESS AND STYLE

Theses two postcards were given away by Morris dealers in their earnest attempts to drive interest in the Cowley (left) and Oxford Traveller estate.

THE MORRIS OXFORD TRAVELLER
THE ALL-PURPOSE VEHICLE THAT'S NEVER OUT OF A JOB!

The Series III Oxford gained new styling with finned tops to the rear wings in 1956; this model famously went into production in India as the Hindustan Ambassador.

Not sure about the event (a French Concours d'Elegance, maybe) or the date but that is French character actor Marcel Dalio patting a very smartly turned out Morris Oxford.

WHO LOVED IT?

These were good, solid motors, firmly rooted in the days when a decent family saloon was neither required to have great acceleration nor be able to cruise at 70mph all day. If you were a Morris person through and through then you would never have considered the Austin A40/A50/A90 series, even though they were dynamically somewhat superior.

the Isis had much in the way of zest (the Cowley was upped to 1.5-litre in 1956), as it could nudge 90mph, but the ride and handling weren't much to write home about on any of them. In various incarnations, including as the Traveller estate, this series was on sale until 1960.

Still, they were tough as old boots. Indeed, so rugged was the Oxford that the 1956 Series III version was chosen for licence-built manufacture in India where, rechristened the Hindustan Ambassador, it is still being made at the time of writing, albeit, I hasten to add, with rather newer, more athletic and less polluting engines.

Fiat 600, 1955

Fiat cars had sold quite well in Britain in the 1930s, and in an even earlier period the company had provided many of the earliest motorised taxi-cabs that replaced London's horse-drawn Hackney carriages. Now the 600 would become the first Italian car, indeed one of the earliest European imports, to make an impression in the post-war 1950s market.

This family car owed some of its inspiration to the Volkswagen format with its engine positioned in the tail, so there was plenty of room for four people in a tiny overall length. But where it diverged from VW's air-cooled practice was in having a water-cooled engine, a compact 633cc unit with four small cylinders.

It took Fiat's chief engineer Dante Giacosa four years to bring to production, during which 300 billion lire was also spent on kitting out the Mirafiori plant in Turin to manufacture it. On top of that, the car was conceived to put the average Italian family on wheels to exploit a massive nationwide road-building programme that would use motorways to open up the whole country.

What they said at the time

'Alpine proving shows again in the gear ratios, and the car is no sluggard up gradients of the order of 1 in 10, such as are met on main roads in Great Britain. The suspension and cornering abilities of this remarkable little car are praiseworthy' – The Autocar magazine in May 1955 on the £585 600.

Economy car, Italian-style: the Fiat 600 was a compact four-seater with its engine at the back, and one of Britain's earliest strong-selling imports.

WHO LOVED IT?

When this car was replaced by the similar 600D, with a bigger engine, in 1960, almost a million examples had been sold. A huge hit in Italy, the 600 was treated with some suspicion by British buyers, who found it a bit too radical and also rather functional. Soon, perhaps, they also realised it was very rust-prone. But there was no doubt it offered affordable motoring for a young family, with a generous dash of Italian style.

Dr Dante Giacosa, the 600's designer and Fiat's creative force, poses with a newly minted 600 outside Fiat's Turin plant in 1959.

Licence-built by SEAT, the 600 also helped to give the peseta-strapped Spanish family its first set of wheels.

Giacosa delivered the 1957 Clayton Lecture at London's Institution of Mechanical Engineers on his development of the 600, which created lots of interest in this unusual car. It was certainly pretty noisy to travel in, but the roadholding was safe. It had an efficient heating and demisting system, and the all-independent suspension made it surprisingly comfortable even on quite rough road surfaces.

By the time the 600 was on UK sale with right-hand drive, a slew of improvements included wind up windows to replace sliding ones. Fiat had also added an unusual six-seater estate car version called the Multipla, which turned out to be a primitive version of what we know today as the MPV, or multi-purpose vehicle; in those days most were pressed into service as compact taxis in Turin and Rome.

Jaguar 2.4-litre, 1955

With this four-door saloon, curvaceous at the front and taperingly sleek at the back with its rear wheels fared in behind neat metal 'spats', Jaguar launched a model that brought its blend of style and performance to a wider market than ever before.

Actually, 'performance' was a bit of a misnomer, as the 2.4-litre six-cylinder car could only just top 100mph, with 0–60mph arriving in 14.4 seconds, on its 112bhp. The engine was a

What they said at the time

'Appreciation begins with the discovery that the driving position, and especially the seat, are exactly right. The delightfully smooth – and silent – performance of the engine is incidentally matched by its shining appearance, and there is evidence of mechanical attention to detail in half-concealed items like the polished dipstick' – The Motor magazine in July 1956 on the £1,532 2.4-litre with overdrive.

smaller, short-stroke edition of the by-now famous XK unit, but this Jag was quite a heavy car: in producing the company's very first monocoque construction vehicle, Jaguar had somewhat over-engineered it to be solid and stable. Still, it beat the pants off an equivalent Rover or Humber for general responsiveness, and its well-resolved suspension front and back provided excellent roadholding by the roly-poly standards of the era.

Inside, with its leather upholstery, polished walnut dashboard, and copious instruments already familiar from other models, it was every inch the Jag. Nonetheless, the standard car came without a rev counter, heater, windscreen washers, fog lights and a cigarette lighter (all of which were included in the Special Equipment edition) to keep the price temptingly competitive. Disc brakes and Borg

Warner automatic transmission arrived as options in 1957.

Appeals for more power were met in 1957 with the 3.4-litre, but this time Jaguar went rather over the top, gifting it with the 210bhp 3.4-litre engine that had previously powered the D-type Le Mans racer. It became a 120mph machine that, until four-wheel disc brakes were fitted in 1958, was something of a handful at high speeds.

It wasn't obvious at the time but this was the first compact and luxurious sports saloon – a car that established the template and ground rules for all such BMWs, Mercs and of course Jaguars to come. Even in this lowliest of editions, it was so much cooler and more capable than a contemporary Rover or Daimler. Just shy of 20,000 examples (as well as about 17,500 3.4s, mostly for export to the USA) were sold up to 1959, at which point the polished Mk 2 successor took compact Jaguars to new heights of desirability.

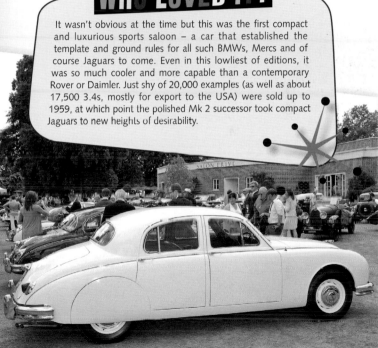

Left: The 2.4-litre was Jaguar's first car without a separate chassis, and its first relatively compact sports saloon.

An immaculate 2.4 photographed recently, showing the rather heavy roofline and small windows that were remedied for the Mk 2.

MGA, 1955

Nobody knew it at the time but the prototype of the MGA was first seen in 1951, when a very similar-looking car put in a manly effort in the Le Mans 24-Hour endurance race. At that time, the staple sports car in MG showrooms was the old-fashioned TD, and that was looking a bit doddery, so it felt like a long wait until the customer-ready MGA finally took its bow in 1955.

The A, though, swiftly recaptured MG's true sports car spirit: it was affordable, stylish and lots of fun.

The alluringly shaped car's new, more rigid chassis hosted a 72bhp version of the British Motor Corporation's 1,489cc 'B' series engine. Its twin carburettors spelt a decent 95mph top speed and 0–60mph in 15.6 seconds. Not as quick as a Triumph TR2, granted, but the MGA was cheaper and felt much more civilised. The 1600 model of 1959 came with a 1,588cc engine, 80bhp and front disc brakes (from 1961), and could brush 100mph, but, while mid-range torque was improved, acceleration was unchanged.

The proper performance fillip came in the form of the MGA Twin Cam of 1958, fitted with a new 1,588cc, 108bhp double-overhead-camshaft engine: over 110mph was now possible, and 0–60mph in a positively blistering 9.1 seconds. It had disc brakes all round and it looked ace, with Dunlop centre-lock disc wheels like the Jaguar D-type's.

Yet the gutsy twin-cam engine was a double-edged sword. It needed high-octane fuel or else the pistons could burn out, and such fuel wasn't common. Worse, it gulped oil like nobody's business. Intended as BMC's main rally car, its temperamental nature led to the Austin-Healey 3000 being used instead. Sales dropped off when the word spread, and the Twin Cam was quietly axed.

In twin-cam form, the MGA was an exciting performance car with a short life due to the fragility of its highly tuned engine.

A 'De Luxe' version was hastily launched to use up surplus disc-braked Twin Cam chassis. Ironically, it's the best MGA of all. And then the 86bhp MGA 1600 Mk II of 1961 increased the 0–60mph time to 13.7 seconds.

The lovely styling and eager performance of the MGA made it an object of desire for any red-blooded 1950s chap.

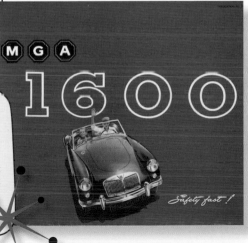

Brochure cover for the later 1600 model exudes sunshine and enjoyment, the left-hand drive indicating these were to be found well away from Britain!

Standard Vanguard Phase III *& Ensign, 1955*

Engineers and designers at Standard-Triumph rolled up their sleeves and got on with hauling the old Vanguard (see p.12) into the modern era. And that meant just about the only component to transfer to the new Phase III unchanged was the rugged 2-litre 68bhp engine, with compression ratio boosted to use the better quality petrol now widely on sale.

This new car lost the separate chassis frame to adopt unitary construction, and was designed around an 8in longer wheelbase so that the rear seat was in front of the rear axle, rather than astride it, and the engine could be moved forward. The result was a saloon or estate that was longer, roomier and lighter. A four-speed gearbox, with overdrive as an option, made it better to drive and did its bit for much better fuel consumption.

There was now a curved, one-piece windscreen although, truth be told, the US-inspired bodywork was no looker, with bulging sides and oddly shaped wheel arches that served to emphasise the big wheels and high ground clearance. Three years after the car was first launched Standard called in Italian coachbuilder Vignale to give the dumpy Vanguard a makeover, and its house designer Giovanni Michelotti worked subtle wonders with a new grille, rear end, bigger windows and chrome accents. Plastic Vynide remained the standard upholstery, with leather available at extra cost; electric screen washers were unusual standard fitments.

Not, perhaps, one of the better looking saloons of its period, the Phase III Vanguard was nonetheless a solid workhorse for a long trip.

The Phase III's all-new structure allowed for rear seats within the wheelbase, providing vastly superior ride comfort compared to the outgoing model.

None of this did anything to improve the car's handling, which was a bit wayward on wet roads, and its stability was easily upset by crosswinds. Disc brakes were never offered.

The basic car led on to a variety of derivatives, including an austere 1.6-litre lookalike called the Ensign, a twin-carb 90bhp Sportsman model, and finally the 1960 Vanguard Luxury Six with an all-new six-cylinder, 2-litre engine that would be used in the much-admired Triumph 2000 in the 1960s.

The 1960 edition of the Vanguard in estate car form; a stylistic makeover by Italian design partners Vignale and Michelotti rendered it considerably more appealing.

Sunbeam Rapier, 1955

Sunbeam was a sports car marque whose glory days, as in independent entity, were back in the 1920s and '30s. Yet the name still had great resonance with enthusiasts in 1950s Britain because post-war cars had been raced and rallied with considerable success.

The Rootes Group, a motor industry giant, had owned Sunbeam since 1935, and these guys were more interested in production numbers than engineering finesse. And the new Rapier sports saloon turned out to be the tip of the iceberg of a new range of models – codenamed Audax – whose big sellers would be the Hillman Minx and Singer Gazelle. The Rapier was revealed at the London Motor Show at Earl's Court in October 1955, preceding the Audax big hitters by several months.

All these cars would share the same basic monocoque structure, but the Sunbeam would be unique in its two-door hardtop design with a 'pillar-less' look when all the side windows were wound down. There were four full seats inside, leather-trimmed, and the characteristic livery was one of several two-tone paint finishes and whitewall tyres – all very on-trend, along with the overall lines, which were suggestive of the latest American Studebakers but on a scale that was more Wallington than Washington.

Despite the column gear change, which was considered the antithesis of sporty but was essential for three people to sit up front, the Rapier was quite spritely. The 1.4-litre, four-cylinder engine with Stromberg carb developed 62.5bhp (updated to twin

This picture was issued by the British Travel & Holidays Association to promote touring in Wales, for which a Sunbeam Rapier could prove ideal.

carburettors in 1957, for 67.5bhp), and overdrive on third and fourth gears was included.

The handling, despite the front anti-roll bar, was none too taut. However, Rootes took the Rapier rallying (one finished fifth on the 1958 Monte Carlo Rally), and the modifications required to make the car competitive meant improvements filtered back to the showroom cars, with the Series II of 1958 more powerful, better-braked, more stiffly sprung and much more exhilarating to drive.

Rootes Group team drivers use Rapiers for practice at the Dunlop Skid Pan in Wolverhampton, prior to the 1958 Monte Carlo Rally.

What they said at the time

'In wet weather there is some wheelspin, as might be expected from the weight distribution, but roadholding is of good saloon standard. The Rapier as a whole feels well balanced with some, but not excessive, oversteer. Those who buy the Rapier for fast motoring will work it hard.' – *The Motor* magazine in March 1957 on the £1,034 Rapier.

1950s
Car Culture

Overwhelmingly British; that was the motoring culture of the post-war period.

The sealed-in, island mentality was inescapable – literally. There had been a car ferry service across the English Channel between Dover and Calais since 1930, when a Captain Townsend converted a minesweeper for the venture. Cars and even coaches had to be craned on and off the craft. In the first year, 6,000 vehicles made the crossing, rising to 31,000 in 1939. Services resumed in 1947, now joined by Southern Railways' Autocarrier, and in 1951 Townsend Brothers' ship was changed to a converted frigate. It was, though, still a service only attainable by the wealthy.

In 1953, after many years of debate and delay, the first roll-on/roll-off car ferries began operation on the route. This was made possible by the building of 'floating bridges' at Dover and at Calais or Boulogne, which allowed vehicles to trundle on and off the ships no matter how high the tide. The built-in margin of 22ft never came

Dover's 'floating bridges' opened in 1953, facilitating the first roll-on/roll-off car ferries to France. Here a Morris Minor, a Humber and two Rovers are about to head off to 'the continent' in 1959 on the *Maid of Kent*.

The quickest way to cross the Channel was by 'air ferry', such as the Silver City service that could cram up to three cars into a converted Bristol Freighter for the 20-minute hop.

An adventurous couple are full of excitement as their Austin A40 Devon is driven into the Silver City Bristol's load bay.

on a 20-minute hop between Lympne in Kent and Le Touquet in France.

Transport Ferry Services increased the options to mainland Europe in 1957 with its roll-on/roll-off ferries between Tilbury and Antwerp.

So it was *possible* to depart the country in your car. But even as late as 1950, there were tough money restrictions. Adults leaving the UK were allowed to take just £50 with them (£35 for children) with a meagre £10 (later £15) extra allowance for running a car, so you wouldn't be going far or for long. Despite being raised to £100, the basic allowance was slashed back to £50 in 1951. In 1952 it was down to £25 and £15 car allowance, which effectively made foreign motoring holidays impossible – to the huge benefit of Britain's seaside B&Bs! Although the rates varied, personal travel restrictions on Sterling would not be lifted entirely until 1959, at which juncture foreign jaunts by car would finally be feasible.

Throughout the 1930s, Britain's carmakers were protected by import tariffs and 'Imperial Preference' measures, but after the war imports were banned, and in 1946 a mere sixty-three foreign cars were registered here, most of them brought in by manufacturers for assessment. By 1949, the figure was 1,868, most being Renaults and Citroëns assembled from imported kits of parts to get around the restriction. Only in spring 1953 were imports

close to being breached, by the way. The 90-minute sea crossing was much swifter without the swinging cranes either side.

And in 1948, Silver City Airways also introduced an air ferry service, with a fleet of Bristol Freighter aircraft converted to fly two or three cars and their passengers

A great overview of the 1948 London Motor Show at Earl's Court, the first such post-war event; a veritable festival of new metal, such as the brand new Sunbeam-Talbots seen in the centre.

This is the 1952 Earl's Court show with the Bentley stand in the foreground, and just beyond that on a raised platform, and sporting whitewall tyres, the all-new Armstrong-Siddeley Sapphire luxury car.

finally allowed and, still hampered by tariffs of up to 30 per cent, Simca, Fiat, Volkswagen and Mercedes-Benz started to offer alternatives to British-made cars. But the impact was tiny: the 10,940 foreign cars sold here in 1958 represented just over 1 per cent of the market.

So although foreign-built cars could be seen at the annual London Motor Show held each October at Earl's Court, these dazzlingly lit events were showcases for the

The public is naturally drawn to the super low price of the new Ford Popular making its debut at Earl's Court in 1953.

Ford's Anglia 100E, despite its archaic engine, is still thought to have been the bestselling car in Britain (official charts weren't published until 1965) throughout the late 1950s.

The Singer SM 1500 Saloon

British car industry. Attendance by people keen to see the latest models from Britain's 'Big Six' manufacturing firms – British Motor Corporation (Austin, Morris, MG, Riley, Wolseley), Rootes Group (Hillman, Humber, Singer, Sunbeam), Ford, Vauxhall, Standard-Triumph and Rover – was enormous. Some 613,000 crowded in there in 1953, an all-time record up to that point.

For years after the war ended, buying a car was near impossible for the average person, even if they had the readies.

In the 1930s, there had been no tax on buying a new car at all. Instead, owners were charged an annual Road Fund Licence tax. The RAC Rating, also known as the Treasury Rating, classified each car based on the surface area of the cylinder bore, having a 'taxation horsepower'

And here's a British car that didn't sell well, the too-expensive Singer SM1500. The marque's dwindling popularity saw it taken over by the Rootes Group in 1956.

Major dealerships offered sales, servicing and parts often on one huge site, such as these Kilburn High Road, north-west London premises of Vauxhall and Bedford agents Hamilton Motors.

Very small numbers of American cars were sold in Britain in the 1950s, such as this Eldorado being handed over outside the showrooms of Cadillac importer Lendrum & Hartman Ltd in Albemarle Street, London W1 in 1956.

Enthusiastic driver Queen Elizabeth II is enjoying herself at the wheel of her Daimler, with Hooper Empress bodywork, on the Windsor estate in 1957. Anne and Charles look bored, though.

Rover broke new ground in creating JET 1, the world's first road-going gas-turbine-powered car; it was a star exhibit at the 1951 Festival of Britain.

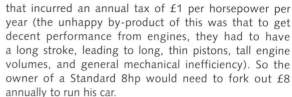

that incurred an annual tax of £1 per horsepower per year (the unhappy by-product of this was that to get decent performance from engines, they had to have a long stroke, leading to long, thin pistons, tall engine volumes, and general mechanical inefficiency). So the owner of a Standard 8hp would need to fork out £8 annually to run his car.

This briefly changed, in 1946, to a simple tax on the cubic capacity of the engine at a rate of £1 per 100cc, which produced a massive outcry from makers of large-engined cars, whose owners were now stung for a huge amount of money every year. Bending to car industry pressure, the government then instituted, from 1 January 1948, a flat-rate road tax of £10 for every car, no matter what its engine size.

It sounded too good to be true of course, and indeed it was. Purchase Tax had been introduced in October 1940 at a rate of 33.3 per cent. Now, in 1947, this was doubled to a swingeing 66.6 per cent on all cars costing £1,000 or more. It spelt disaster for makers of luxury cars; a £1,270 Daimler DB18 would now cost £1,977 on the road.

In 1951, Purchase Tax on all new cars was raised to 66.6 per cent. Although it fell to 50 per cent in 1952 it was back up to 60 per cent in 1955, reverting to

Above: The 1953 film *Genevieve* packed out cinemas, and put old car enthusiasm firmly in the public consciousness.

Left: Banger racing arrived in 1952, and helped to clear the streets of spent jalopies, such as this one campaigned by famous north London second-hand car dealer Raymond Way Motors.

The kit car craze began when replacement glass-fibre bodies could breathe new life into rusted-out or crash-damaged old Fords and Austins; this Tornado Typhoon utilised old parts in an all-new chassis too.

Kids were car-mad in the 1950s, and this House of Storey birthday card would have brought a grin to any five-year-old on his big day … especially if there was a 10 shilling note tucked inside it.

50 per cent in 1959 as the government used it as a blunt instrument to regulate demand; contrast that with the VAT rate of 20 per cent in the early twenty-first century.

Right into the 1950s, there were wartime-style restrictions on car purchase. To begin with, only drivers with a pressing need for a car were actually sanctioned to purchase one, and after that buyers had to sign a covenant promising that they wouldn't sell on their new cars at inflated prices in a black market until after a given period. Most of this kind of thing had been swept away by 1953, although it wasn't until 1958 that tight rules about hire purchase (we call it car finance these days),

such as the need for a deposit of at least 50 per cent, were dropped.

Most of these measures, incidentally, had been designed to encourage export sales rather than home market ones, in Britain's struggle to earn foreign currency and pay off the nation's wartime debts.

Cars new and old were causing a stir in the early 1950s. There was a tantalising glimpse into a possible motoring future from Rover with the unveiling of JET 1, the world's first road-going vehicle with a gas turbine engine. It was one of the most popular exhibits at the 1951 Festival of Britain on London's South Bank; it shared

An Austin J40 pedal car made an exceptional birthday present for any budding driver, such as young Tim here; they were introduced in 1949 by Austin, and built by disabled workers in a South Wales factory.

the Transport Pavilion with, among others, Lt Col. A.T. 'Goldie' Gardner's streamlined MG speed record car, and a Hillman Minx with totally transparent plastic bodywork. Meanwhile, Lord Edward Montagu opened an innovative 'motor museum' at his family seat in Beaulieu, Hampshire in 1952 – in fact, it began with five veteran cars wheeled into the stately pile's entrance hall, and visitors proved to be enchanted by these venerable motoring pioneers. The following year, *Genevieve* was released at the cinema, in glorious colour, a feel-good movie following rival drivers,

and their other halves, as they battled to Brighton and back on the Veteran Car Run. It all signalled the start of restoring and driving old cars as a hobby, although for motors that were just old as opposed to very, very old, the immediate future was bleak after banger racing was introduced at London's New Cross Stadium on Good Friday, 1952. More than 26,000 people saw big old American cars wreck one another; the automotive carnage since has reduced survival of many sturdy classics to penny numbers.

Another trend was the kit car, usually in the form of a plastic sports car body that could add new life to an Austin Seven or Ford Y-Type where the bodywork was rusty or crash damaged but the chassis still serviceable. Early brands designed so you could build your own sporty 'special' at home on a shoestring budget were Ashley, Buckler, Rochdale and Tornado.

However, the one type of car to make a real impact on the roads of Britain this decade was the 'bubble car'. With petrol rationing and the threat of fuel scarcity because of the Suez crisis, these tiny three- and four-wheelers from Germany, including the BMW Isetta, Messerschmitt, Heinkel, Goggomobil and Fuldamobil, with their motorcycle engines and minimal running costs, became familiar sights. There were some British ones too, such as the Scootacar, Coronet, Powerdive and Opperman Unicar, as well as the surprisingly popular Bond Minicar. In fact, demand for them was for a while so strong that the British Motor Corporation took note, and decided to beat them at their own game with a 'real car in miniature'. That would be the Mini, which dominated the following decade, and killed off the bubble cars entirely.

The bubble cars needed a degree of re-learning to drive. It wasn't always easy to get any driving tuition, especially after paid lessons were banned during the Suez Crisis when examiners were roped in to help manage the scrum of rationing at petrol stations. Drivers on provisional licences – get this – were allowed at this time to drive unaccompanied. Just before the crisis, the test fee had doubled from 10s to £1.

Learner drivers started the decade poorly, with 50 per cent failing the test at their first try in 1950. And only in 1959 was driving examiner training standardised to a formula devised by the Stanmore Training School. 'We are often asked how long it will take to bring a pupil up to test standard,' said the British School of Motoring in a 1952 booklet which emphasised its sixty-five branches, same rate for daytime or evening lessons, and Patent Safety Dual Control System. 'This depends entirely upon the pupil's temperament and ability to learn.'

In 1960, its chief instructor F.R. Priestley issued '30 Tips On Better Driving', which included such starchy gems as: 'Make good use of sun shadows, reflections in shop windows, and remember that the driving mirror is your third eye; use it every six seconds'; and: 'Never drive with your arm resting on the window; you need both arms poised to deal with an emergency, e.g. burst tyre, avoiding action.' It does all seem a long time ago …

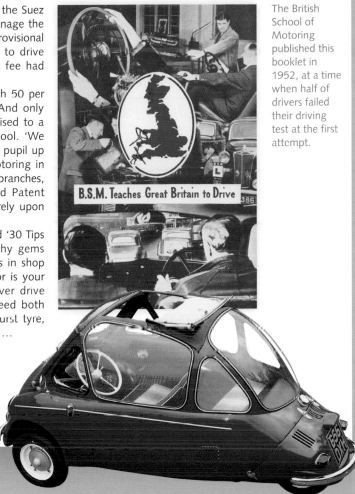

The British School of Motoring published this booklet in 1952, at a time when half of drivers failed their driving test at the first attempt.

B.S.M. Teaches Great Britain to Drive

Britain went mad for bubble cars in the fuel scare caused by the Suez Crisis, and many were imported from Germany, such as this Heinkel Cabin Cruiser.

Ford Consul, Zephyr & Zodiac Mk II, 1956

Ford of Britain's Mk II range of large saloons was so crucial to the company that it hired the huge Harringay Stadium in which to launch the car on 21 February 1956, packing the place with VIP guests from all over the world.

They gathered to celebrate the maturing of the Consul, Zephyr and Zodiac as they became the epitome of modern family motoring. The tagline for the new range was 'The Three Graces' for their wider, longer, sleeker lines over an extended wheelbase compared to the outgoing cars. Brits could be a bit sniffy about 'Americanism', but the consensus was that these saloons captured just enough Detroit style to make them handsome without being over-ornate.

The four-cylinder Consul, with the thinner front grille, saw the biggest change, with an engine capacity boost to 1.7 litres. For the six-cylinder Zephyr and its gaudy running mate the Zodiac, the 2.6-litre engine behind the bigger grille was carried over.

Extensive prototype testing had led to a smaller turning circle and better weight distribution. Once it was rolling off the Dagenham production line, tyre-maker Goodyear ran a Zephyr Mk II for a continuous twenty-month trial to test its rubber; it averaged 50mph over the 410,000 miles covered … although it did have to have two new engines along the way. Still, the first replacement wasn't needed until the car hit 158,000 miles, and the 86bhp Zephyr acquitted itself in saloon car racing, and police forces liked it as a rapid patrol car.

A few months after launch, the car's image was properly boosted when convertible models joined the range, any of which could be ordered with a power-operated hood, and there was also an estate car with a side-opening tailgate.

Ford never let the cars go stale, offering an automatic gearbox in late 1956, overdrive on the manual gearbox in 1957, a lower roofline in 1959 to keep the car looking modern, and front disc brakes as an option in 1960 and standard in '61.

An open-air debrief on the finer points of the Mk II models of Consul, Zephyr and Zodiac underway at the Ford Dagenham headquarters.

'One of the greatest impressions this new Ford made on drivers (who had recently handled the earlier model) was by its roadability. Longer, wider, lower and with the weight better distributed – all these changes are reflected in the cornering and the roadholding' – *The Autocar* magazine in April 1956 on the £872 Zephyr.

The Consul was the four-cylinder edition, with a 1.7-litre engine, in a three-car range entitled 'The Three Graces'.

The Mk II, seen here as a Zodiac convertible, was certainly a handsome car, adapting American lines to a British scale.

WHO LOVED IT?

It says a lot about the cars' popularity that the convertible and estate models had to be converted by outside companies; such was the demand for these cars that Ford couldn't afford to slow the production line to cope with low-volume variations! They built 680,000 of them until 1962; the 371,000 Consuls alone showed how rivals like the Standard Vanguard were swept aside by the Ford bandwagon.

Hillman Minx, 1956

The Minx was never really an innovator, and that applied from the time the catchy name first lit up the car market in 1932 to the moment it petered out in 1970. But that didn't stop the Rootes Group's Coventry factories from churning out these solid family cars, whose design was constantly updated, in their tens of thousands every year.

They stayed well back from the cutting edge of automotive technology but offered predictable, workaday motoring – compact saloons that were reasonably reliable, fashionable, and good value.

There had already been eight generations of 'Phase' models before this new car, and the codename Audax series, begun with the closely related Sunbeam Rapier (see p. 120), became the first of five 'Series' cars. The engine had already been modernised with overhead-valve design in 1954, and now the Series I of 1956 ushered in sculpted new styling and a much roomier interior. In fact, Rootes had paid American design consultants the Loewy Organisation to help them make the Minx irresistible to buyers, which partly explains the

wraparound rear window and the two-tone paint jobs.

Rootes unfolded a huge range to choose from, with the new Minx offered in Special and De Luxe forms, as an estate, as a convertible, in a more elaborate livery as the Singer Gazelle, and as a basic van-like station wagon called the Husky. The four-speed gearbox had either

This convertible of the all-new Minx was the rarest edition; note the generous four-seater accommodation.

The Minx family came to be stitched into the fabric of Britain's roadscape and, as second-hand cars, permitted many families to move up to something bigger and better for the first time. There was little in the manner of driving scintillation to be had from them, but they were dependable and mechanically very straightforward.

What they said at the time

'Practical and pleasing, for passengers as well as for the driver. In its latest form, faster and more comfortable, as well as roomier and better looking, the Hillman Minx seems likely to prove even more popular than hitherto' – *The Motor* magazine in May 1956 on the £773 Minx De Luxe.

A Special saloon with 1.5-litre engine, in 1959, continuing the Minx tradition of roomy but economical mid-range family cars.

Part-finished bodies for the Minx and Husky making their way by road from the Pressed Steel factory to Hillman's Coventry assembly plant.

a steering column or floor-mounted lever, and the early cars offered a Lockheed clutchless semi-automatic option called, unsurprisingly, the Manumatic. This basic range lasted until 1967, with annual tinkering from designers to keep the cars up to date, which saw tail fins come and go and the engine size swell from 1.4 litres to 1.7 litres.

Metropolitan, 1956

Nash Motors of Kenosha, Wisconsin, USA had been toying with the idea of a really small 'sub-compact' car since the end of the Second World War. It was convinced that a good market lay in store among affluent US families for a 'second car' that the lady of the house would use principally for shopping – a reflection of changing American demographics as the suburbs spread.

Independent Detroit designer William Flajole was asked to produce a design study, the NXI (Nash Experimental International), and then Nash took the novel step of using market researchers to canvass the public on its views at a series of specially organised events in 1949.

Potential buyers loved it, but said they would only go for one if it was cheap to buy and run. Nash had no experience in building economical vehicles, and so it turned to a company that did: our very own Austin. The British company had the ideal 1.2-litre engine and three-speed gearbox, from the A40 Somerset, for immediate use, and was aching to find a successful export product for the US market.

The companies were ideal joint-venture partners, and manufacture of the Nash Metropolitan began in October 1953, the smart-looking little car going on sale six months later exclusively in the USA and Canada. The marketing campaign was aimed directly at housewives. It came as a two-door convertible or hardtop, and a radio and heater were fitted to every car. In 1956, a larger 1.5-litre engine accompanied numerous detail improvements, although top speed remained slothful, at just 75mph.

From April 1957 Nash allowed Austin to sell the Metropolitan in Britain too, where its vibrant two-tone colour schemes and transatlantic looks really set it apart ... as did its dreadful turning circle and a generally vague and unresponsive feel to its steering, cornering and braking. Corny singing star Alma Cogan was a natural customer.

An externally opening boot lid belatedly appeared in 1959, its best American year, when 22,209 were sold. This made it the second bestselling import after the Volkswagen Beetle.

Cover of the brochure for UK marketing of the Metropolitan; the colourful three-seater made quite an impression here.

Jazzy upholstery and plenty of legroom for three; this one is heading for the USA or Canada, the destination for most of these quirky Anglo-American machines.

A convertible model being hotly debated by two car enthusiasts; from this angle you can rather see why the car had a rotten turning circle …

WHO LOVED IT?

Austin did sterling business with the Metropolitan venture by building 104,377 examples up to 1961, with the lion's share of these (94,986) destined for US/Canadian export. It was odd that no direct replacement for this important British export success ever materialised. In this country, the car made quite a statement about you as being into the very latest fads – like a bright pink Fiat 500 might today.

Renault Dauphine, 1956

Renault intended to offer a step up from the 4CV for its many loyal customers and chose the name Dauphine – meaning heiress – for that very aspirational purpose. The company spent four years testing prototypes to ensure they got the car just right.

In the 4CV vein, it was a rear-engined four-door saloon, with the engine being an enlarged 845cc version of the 4CV's well-proven water-cooled, four-cylinder motor. There, though, the similarity ended. The Dauphine featured pretty styling, with a well-defined 'boot' at the back in contrast to the 4CV's slope back. The wheelbase was 6in longer, so it was much roomier inside, and the doors were front-hinged, unlike the 'suicide' doors on the 4CV. The interior featured a red-and-black theme that even extended to the steering wheel.

One of the car's key boasts was its 45mpg fuel economy. This was certainly a more admirable asset than its handling, which with its rear weight bias could be a bit frightening in the wet, as the 34bhp engine was quite powerful in a relatively light and tinny car. But that was no bar to tuning firm Gordini, which extracted 38bhp from the car, making a four-speed gearbox standard in 1958 and creating a sparkling race and rally car in the process … when piloted in skilled hands. Acceleration was hugely better, and there was a green-and-black steering wheel to mark it out.

Renault's factories could barely keep up with demand, pumping out a Dauphine every twenty-five seconds. It supplied kits of parts for cars to be assembled in Acton, West London, to beat import duties, which made up a few of the 43 per cent of Dauphines exported.

What they said at the time

'Thanks to its flat floor, the Dauphine is a quite genuine four-seater. There is exceptionally little body roll during fast cornering, and the tail-heavy feeling of earlier rear-engined Renaults seems to have been overcome' – The Motor magazine in January 1957 on the £769 Dauphine.

The pretty Dauphine extended the rear-engined theme from the 760/4CV but with more comfort and panache.

After visiting the Renault factory at Flins, HRH the Queen was given a powder-blue – but British-assembled – Dauphine as a gift from Renault.

WHO LOVED IT?

Renault stopped making this car in December 1967, by which time it had shifted 2,150,738 Dauphines. It did quite well in the UK, including one order for 800 red examples, which formed the fleet of Welbeck Motors, London's first major minicab company – leading to much animosity, and several intimidating confrontations, from the capital's black cab drivers in 1958.

Above: The 'bonnet' tipped forward to offer commodious luggage space in the car, although most long holidays for four would probably have demanded a roof rack too.

Humber Hawk & SuperSnipe, 1957

The Rootes Group embarked on an all-out assault on the executive/luxury car market in 1957. To achieve this it designed a totally new unitary-construction hull, Britain's biggest of its day, which could be used for both the four-cylinder Hawk and the six-cylinder Super Snipe. For styling inspiration, as ever, it turned to the USA, picking what it considered the most modern elements of mid-1950s sedans from Chevrolet, Hudson and Plymouth to massage into the saloon style and, unusually, station wagon body options.

The 2.3-litre Hawk came first in 1957, followed a year later by the 2.6-litre Super Snipe. Both cars could be had as an estate, its tailgate split into a drop-down lower section that elongated the loadspace and a lift-up rear window.

Overdrive was optional on the Hawk, but automatics were mostly reserved for the Snipe. Neither handled well, tending to wallow around alarmingly on corners, and disc front brakes were a welcome improvement by 1960.

Also that year, the Snipe scored a minor 'first' with the fitment of Britain's first four-headlamp system, with much encouragement from Lucas, which made the lights! The car received a new 3-litre engine, too, which endowed it with a relaxed and quiet 100mph performance.

These were competent cars, if not especially accomplished ones, but as the 1960s wore on Rootes hesitated to replace them as sales dwindled, and when the last ones were built in 1967 the era of the big Humbers finished on a whimper.

This gaudy-looking Humber Hawk featured a 2.3-litre overhead-valve engine.

The Super Snipe estate car showing off its split tailgate, and the deft feature of a top-hinged number plate and light.

WHO LOVED IT?

Big Humbers basked in a reputation for power and stamina that could be traced back to the cars that General Montgomery drove in the Second World War. In the decades that followed, they tended to be favoured by officialdom for their combination of space and value; these attributes were certainly present in this new model range, but when sales were eaten into by Rover and Jaguar, the wind was taken from Humber's sales, and Rootes eventually gave up on them.

'Ouch!', or perhaps a stronger expletive, was likely uttered by the driver when this Hawk, undergoing durability tests at the Motor Industry Research Association, came back to earth.

BMW Isetta, 1957

The Isetta is the original bubble car, and it's easy to see why when you clock its tiny, egg-like form.

The design originated in Italy in 1953, where the ISO refrigerator and scooter company planned it as a step up from a two-wheeler – city transport with weather protection and four wheels, the rear two positioned just 19in apart, and a single door forming the car's entire frontage, hinged at one side, with a steering column that snapped into place when it was closed. Despite carrying two adults and a child, this 'cabin scooter' wasn't very popular, most potential buyers preferring a Fiat 500C.

Meanwhile, BMW felt the Isetta could help reverse its sinking fortunes, and took out a licence to make it in Munich. In fact, in 1955 it acquired all the tooling from Italy, installed its own single-cylinder motorcycle engine, and added numerous design improvements.

BMW in turn granted a licence to Isetta of Great Britain, and two years later the car was being manufactured, using many locally sourced components, in an old railway locomotive factory just outside Brighton.

This was the BMW Isetta 300 model, with engine enlarged to 295cc and 13bhp, so the tiny (7.5ft long) car could manage 53mph and tackle even steep gradients without running out of puff. The gearbox was a manual four-speeder, and a combination Dynastart starter-generator kicked it into life. The Isetta now boasted sliding side windows too. In providing right-hand drive, though, the driving position was now on the same side as the engine, so a 60lb cast-iron counterweight was installed to make sure the car didn't topple over.

UK sales were slow until the Isetta was redesigned with a single wheel at the back. It reverted briefly to left-hand drive for safe weight distribution, but a right-hooker with requisite ballast did finally emerge.

WHO LOVED IT?

In the bubble car's short golden era before the Fiat Nuova 500 and Mini killed them off, the BMW Isetta was one of the most popular, with more than 161,000 made in Germany until 1962, plus a rather astonishing 30,000 from Brighton for UK and Commonwealth market sales. It only did well in the UK as a three-wheeler because it attracted much lower tax rates as a tricycle. If the reverse gear was blocked off, it could also be driven on a provisional motorbike licence! The NHS issued a few to wheelchair-bound drivers for their ease of access.

Below: The face of the BMW Isetta 250, 1955; the little car would go on to be built in Brighton, where a three-wheeler model was developed.

What they said at the time

'The human factor is really the one which would normally limit the car to local or suburban use. Gentle cruising, or main road work with a following wind are comparatively restful, but a strong headwind has a pronounced effect on performance, and the noise rises accordingly' – *The Motor* magazine in March 1957 on the £389 BMW Isetta 300.

Above: Yes, that really is suave Cary Grant in New York proving that the little BMW Isetta was the coolest city runabout around.

Left: The Standard, on the left, and Export Isettas as manufactured by BMW from the original Italian design.

Riley 1.5 & Wolseley 1500, 1957

This pair of attractive compact saloons, which were near-identical, wore their respective identities with pride.

The Wolseley was a willing performer with its 48bhp BMC B Series four-cylinder engine, but the Riley was positively peppy with 68bhp, thanks to its twin SU carburettors. That meant it could power on to 85mph, and it made a decent little saloon car racer in its day.

In all other respects, and badges apart, the two cars shared most other elements. This started with the fundamentals because they both used the Morris Minor floorpan, suspension and steering, which

made them just as good to drive as that satisfying small car. The Riley, however, had bigger, beefier brakes.

Internally, meanwhile, the cabins were pleasantly and invitingly trimmed with leather-faced seats and a wooden dashboard (the Riley's boasting a rev-counter).

It all seemed like a lot of trouble to go to in order to create new cars for BMC's already crowded range. Yet this was the era of multiple sales networks, which all demanded their own cars to sell, and Riley and Wolseley agents were vocal in

their insistence that they needed dedicated new models to keep their customers loyal. Hence, the British Motor Corporation became the masters of 'badge engineering', where one design was sold in several different guises. The Wolseley and Riley pairings at most price levels were generally very similar, with Rileys being given a slight edge in performance as befitted that particular make's heritage.

The Riley 1.5 was a peppy little car, with sporting responses thanks to its twin-carburettor power unit.

The Wolseley 1500 was angled more towards luxury and style, but thanks to its Morris Minor underpinnings was still good to drive.

What they said at the time

'Entering a corner fast, one has the feeling of the car collecting itself – taking up the slack – in a way which, although it may seem a far-fetched parallel, is reminiscent of the procedure used by the equestrian at a fence' – *The Autocar* in November 1957 on the £863 Riley 1.5.

WHO LOVED IT?

These cars reached out beyond the confines of the existing Riley and Wolseley customer base. If anyone wanted a Morris Minor but with more performance and a great deal of extra cabin ambience, they had what it took. Production ended in 1965, with almost 40,000 Rileys and just over 103,000 Wolseleys sold.

Vauxhall Velox & Cresta PA Series, 1957

It was with capturing a slice of US glamour in mind that the unitary-construction PA took shape in Vauxhall's Luton design centre from 1955. The new cars had long, sleek lines, with fashionable fins topping off the rear wings, bold rear light clusters and lustrous chrome trim tracing the outline of the low-set grille and headlights. Most remarkable was the windscreen. It wrapped around the sides of the car to give a truly panoramic view out, while at the back a novel three-piece rear window provided outstanding all-round visibility.

With gear lever mounted on the steering column and full-width bench seats in the back *and* the front, the new cars could accommodate six adults comfortably.

The familiar 2.2-litre six-cylinder engine was carried over from previous Vauxhalls. This gutsy power unit, mated to a three-speed manual gearbox meant the car hit 60mph in 16 seconds and had an 89mph top speed – not bad in those just pre-motorway times.

Steering was light and the road-holding excellent by contemporary standards. And the Velox and, more especially, the opulent Cresta added some much-needed colour and style to Britain's roads. There was a raft of striking two-tone paint jobs, or you could order something simpler but just as vivid, like bright pink or apple green. The Cresta sported whitewall tyres and anodised hubcaps just like its American cousins, while upholstery could be in two-tone leather, herringbone-weave Nylon – still then a wonder material – or hardwearing 'Elastofab'.

The company worked on the PA's shortcomings. A new grille and a wraparound single-piece rear window

Just imagine the impact that these flash new Vauxhall PA models, shown off here in glorious Cresta form, made on Britain's drab roadscape …

to match the front one were new for 1960, plus an engine boost to 2.6 litres, and optional overdrive, giving 96mph top speed. Wheels grew from 13 to 14in. A roomy estate version was also offered. A couple of months later came the option of automatic transmission, while 1962 cars boasted servo-assisted front disc brakes.

WHO LOVED IT?

By the time the car was replaced by the modern but altogether less spectacular PB range in 1962, 173,604 PAs had been made. Vauxhall's two-millionth vehicle, built in February 1959, was in fact a PA Cresta. Thousands were exported as far afield as Australia and Canada, but at home the ritzy Cresta was just about the trendiest new car you could buy in 1957.

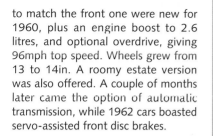

The chrome-laden frontage of the PA Cresta might have evoked the excesses of Detroit, but buyers loved it!

It's Her Car-Mad Majesty once more, this time in her own beloved Cresta PA estate with its particularly appropriate personal number plate.

What they said at the time

'It's big, yet not so bulky as to be a nuisance around towns which date back to pre-motoring days, lively and fast yet by no means expensive to run, and offering quite a high standard of refinement' – *The Motor* magazine in April 1958 on the £1,073 Cresta.

Vauxhall Victor F-type, 1957

This all-new car completed Vauxhall's total range overhaul in 1957. Like the bigger Velox and Cresta, its styling was heavily influenced by then-current trends in Detroit, with its whole design strongly redolent of Chevrolet's iconic 1957 Bel Air range.

Opinion was divided as to whether this worked or not, especially as the 13in wheels looked a bit mean with all that sculpted metal around them. Other faddish touches were the wrap-around front and rear screens and an exhaust tailpipe that stuck out through a stylised part of the back bumper.

The 1.5-litre four-cylinder engine was a comprehensive rework of the unit in the old Wyvern that the Victor replaced, a 48bhp motor with single Zenith carburettor and a raised compression ratio so that it could run sweetly on the 'premium' grade petrol that was now widely available. With a four-speed all-synchromesh gearbox, this made for a responsive and rugged drivetrain. The column-mounted gear change, while disliked by some drivers, meant a three-seater front bench could be installed.

In 1958, the launch of the factory-built Victor estate caused quite a stir, for it was Vauxhall's first. Yet only a year later the Victor range was face-lifted, its Series II styling considerably toned-down and its engine power upped to 55bhp to cope with the upcoming motorway age. A new De Luxe range-topper came with leather upholstery and bucket front seats.

Inside, all these Victors had trendy two-tone interiors with upholstery in Rayon or stretchy 'Elastofab', and a slew of convenience features like armrests on the doors, a door-operated courtesy light and twin sun visors.

A practical and spacious Victor F-type estate playing its part in the 1950s rebuilding of Britain.

Below: The early Victor had a lot to recommend it in terms of space and comfort, but its poor durability was its Achilles heel.

Below right: As this cherubic young lady demonstrates, the wraparound windscreen brought much joy to motoring families across the land.

WHO LOVED IT?

Initial demand for this new Vauxhall was huge, but the strong start in home and export sales, especially to the USA where it was sold through Pontiac dealers, soon hit the skids when the Victor's design faults (down to hasty development) showed themselves: a tendency to rust badly, water leaks around those curved screens, and weak structural design, which meant doors and bonnet would soon not close properly. But Vauxhall still managed to sell an impressive 390,000 of the first F-types, and the mechanical parts were unbreakable.

What they said at the time

'The engine is not obtrusive and the Victor will cruise happily in the middle sixties when the driver is in a hurry. Less likeable, there is a slight vibration period extending from about 47mph to 55mph, and this seems to be amplified by the body shell so what should be a particularly effortless part of the speed range is, in fact, its least happy pace' – The Motor magazine in March 1957 on the £758 Victor Super.

6549 AH

Into the 1960s

With just four months of the 1950s left to go, in August 1959 the wraps came off one of the most technically significant cars of the late twentieth century. The Mini was revealed, and the whole world was agog.

The tiny four-seater saloon would have no bearing on 1950s motoring. That's why it doesn't appear on previous pages, along with other cars launched in the very late 1950s that would only make their mark in the following decade. They were born in the era covered by this book but wholly relevant to the following one, which is the rationale for this chapter.

The Mini, marketed initially as either an Austin Se7en or Morris Mini-Minor by the British Motor Corporation, had its roots in the Suez Crisis that so spooked the country (and shattered its grandiose world view of itself) in the mid 1950s. As a direct response to scarce fuel supplies, sales of tiny 'bubble cars' suddenly took off and captured the public's imagination. In turn, BMC took a long hard look at what it considered inadequate little machines and decided that it would make a 'real car in miniature'. The task was assigned to maverick engineer-designer Alec Issigonis.

The bubbles, many of which as three-wheelers were, legally, lumped in with motorbikes, could mostly carry two adults in cramped conditions, with space for perhaps one or two toddlers to squeeze in. But the Mini could take four adults within its tiny 10ft length. This was because Issigonis created a compact front-wheel-drive powerpack, with the gearbox tucked underneath inside the oil sump, as well as rubber cone suspension and small wheels,

The Mini, seen here in its original Austin version, really was the wonder car of the new decade, easily able to carry four adults within its 10ft length.

Morris dealers got their own version of the Mini, called the Mini-Minor, with just as much fanfare made about its novel attributes.

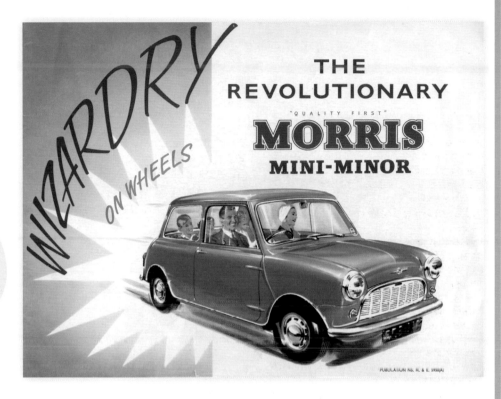

THE REVOLUTIONARY

"QUALITY FIRST"

MORRIS MINI-MINOR

which robbed the car of the least interior space, and storage in door pockets and on the shelf that replaced a conventional dashboard to compensate for the restricted boot space.

All this practical stuff, together with the artificially low price, was admirable. But the best part about the car was the way it drove. With a wheel at each corner and front-wheel drive, it was agile and safe, tending towards go-kart levels of driving thrills even at relatively low speeds. The performance potential that was manifest would lead to the zippy Mini Cooper, while the car's cheeky looks gave it classless appeal.

Yet the Mini was by no means the only attractive small car launched in 1959 that would soon be commonplace.

The Herald was Triumph's interesting entry into the small car market, with styling provided by Italian genius Giovanni Michelotti.

There was also the Triumph Herald, with its smart Italian styling and its separate chassis construction leading to a wide choice of body styles; it boasted low running costs and its 25ft turning circle made it a nimble town car. And there was the natty Ford Anglia 105E, with its rev-happy overhead-valve engine and four-speed gearbox – Ford's first for Britain – providing genuine driving enjoyment.

A few years further away, in 1963, were the belated small car responses from Rootes Group and Vauxhall, both of which came from brand new, specially built factories.

Long before the *Harry Potter* books and movies made it world-famous, the Anglia 105E was one of the best-loved British economy cars of the 1960s.

The Hillman Imp of 1963 had a lot to recommend it, not least its space and practicality, but it never achieved anything like the Mini's popularity.

The Viva HA was a huge hit with the ladies – indeed, that's who Vauxhall marketed it to, with its easy-to-drive nature.

Rootes' Hillman Imp, manufactured in Scotland, was the more adventurous, with its rear-mounted, all-aluminium engine allowing for a roomy interior, an opening 'hatchback' back window making it good for shopping errands, and sharp-edged styling inspired by US and Italian trends. In contrast, Vauxhall's new Viva of 1963 – hailing from the spanking new Ellesmere Port plant – was

AUSTIN HEALEY

Sprite

Above: Front cover of the brochure for the Austin-Healey Sprite, showing off the cheeky appearance that earned it the 'Frogeye' nickname.

Left: Ford's first Cortina was a huge and instant hit, representing excellent value for money and well able to cope with constantly high-speed motorway driving.

The Sunbeam Alpine was a terrific addition to Britain's sports car ranks, offering style, performance, comfort and two little back seats for kids, or dogs!

utterly conventional, like a scaled-down Victor, with front engine and rear drive, but the hardware was well proven, the design neat, the boot big and the driving experience very easy. Vauxhall targeted the car at female customers, an important new buyer stratum just then emerging, and the Viva proved a spectacular success.

One size up would be Ford's 1962 Cortina. It was a machine of both the consumer and motorway ages,

Daimler briefly joined in with Britain's 1960s sports car explosion with its SP250, featuring an excellent 2.5-litre V8 engine.

Big 3-litre engines were to feature in Austin-Healeys during the 1960s; the car won fans and rallies in equal measure.

The transformation from 'Mk I' (see p. 114) to this Mk 2 created the seminal compact sports saloon of the 1960s ... and BMW took note for the future.

Not quite the car for Mr Bond (that would be the subsequent DB5), yet the DB4 remained a super-desirable possession for those with money, verve and taste.

offering a great deal of car for the money, masses of model choice, and light yet strong construction using well-proven components that made it ideal for sustained high average speeds on the new multi-lane highway network that would rapidly take shape during the 1960s. Indeed, the Cortina did most to show up the inadequacies of 1950s family cars, which had never been designed to cruise all day at 70mph on motorways, and were apt to overheat, seize up, come apart or conk out if pressed to do so.

Britain was the world centre for affordable sports car manufacture, with its MGs, Triumphs and Austin-Healeys finding favour all over the world, and the more specialised Lotuses, Morgans, Turners, Berkeleys and Rochdales serving very dedicated enthusiasts at home.

There were two important new additions to this fun car line-up in the late 1950s. The most significant was the 1958 Austin-Healey Sprite, a little gem of a two-seater with monocoque construction, a 948cc engine, and a front end that lifted up in one unit and featured headlights on the bonnet top that led to its 'Frogeye' nickname. The mechanical parts were a happy cocktail of Austin A35 and Morris Minor, and the irresistibly low price of £679 was made possible by leaving out anything that wasn't key to driving enjoyment, such as a rear boot lid!

In 1959, the Rootes Group barged into the sports car big league with its Sunbeam Alpine. As with other popular models, the mechanical parts weren't exotic, being gathered from other Hillman models in the Rootes catalogue, but the 1.5-litre engine gave a rousing 83bhp thanks to various modifications including an aluminium cylinder head, and its distinctive rear fins were part of a very stylish look. Two-plus-two seating and an excellent hood completed an alluring package.

We shouldn't forget, either, the highly individual Daimler SP250, with its glass-fibre bodywork and delightful V8 engine, nor the first of the big-engined Austin-Healey 3000s – both making their debut in late 1959. As the 1960s progressed more classic sports cars would arrive, including the Lotus Elan, MGB and Triumph Spitfire. But even before the new decade began, Jaguar was redefining the sports saloon with its Mk 2.

The Mk 1 (a retrospective title) range had several flaws, but the new car fixed them all with its all-round disc brakes, wider track, clever design tweaks and an interior made more pleasant by bigger windows and rear screen. The option of a bigger 3.8-litre straight-six XK engine turned it into a road-burning 125mph express. With its stablemates, the sensational E-type sports car and the awesome Mark X luxury car, the Mk 2 would make the 1960s a golden era for this great British marque.

And what if your car funds were limitless and you could pick something from the very top drawer? Well, you might have been drawn naturally to the truly beautiful Aston Martin DB4, new for 1958, with its all-new 4-litre straight-six engine and to-die-for fastback GT lines by Touring of Milan. Or the Bristol 406 of that year, with its totally new body style and equally handmade aura. And right at the top of the tree were the Bentley S2 and Rolls-Royce Silver Cloud II – and their raffish Continental sporting spin-offs – featuring the all-new Rolls-Bentley V8 engine at a magnificent 6.3 litres. Fully recognising the cars were increasingly likely to be driven by their owners, rather than the chauffeurs of old, these Rollers and Bentleys all came with automatic transmission and power steering as standard.

The Ford Zodiac Mk II, introduced in 1956, was one of the best large family cars you could buy – solidly built, reliable, decent to drive and stylishly modern.